HIT AND RUN TRADING

The Short-Term Stock Traders' Bible

Jeff Cooper

M. GORDON PUBLISHING GROUP
Malibu, California

First printing October 1996
Second printing December 1996
Third printing March 1997
Fourth printing October 1997
Fifth printing February 1998
Sixth printing August 1999

ISBN 0-9650461-2-5

Printed in the United States of America

To my wife Suzie, my father Jack,
and in memory of my mother Josephine.

Disclaimer

Past results are not indicative of future returns. The publisher, the author, and their affiliates make no claim to the future effectiveness of the methods described in this book. Examples in this book are for educational purposes only. This is not a solicitation of any order to buy or sell.

CONTENTS

● ●

ACKNOWLEDGMENTS

■ ■

To my editor Bill Masciarelli, for helping make my manuscript a cohesive work.

To Bob Pisani, Tony Winecoff, Dr. Joseph Bassett, Pam Gipson, and Danilo Torres for taking time out of their busy schedules to proofread the book.

To Judy Brown of Brown Enterprises in Woodstock, Illinois, for doing a great job on the layout and design and to David Kojimoto of Progression, Inc. in Los Angeles, California, for creating a wonderful book cover.

I would also like to thank Michael Berger of Manhattan Investment Fund, David Reif of Patterson Icenogle, Mike Jenkins of Stock Cycles Forecast, Mike Bradley of Pro-Active Investor, and Ed Kasanjian of Kasanjian Research who over the years have taken the time to share their ideas and market insights.

And especially to Larry Connors, the inspiration behind this work.

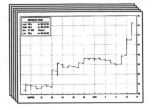

CHAPTER 1

THE OPENING BELL

. . . .

It's not whether you get knocked down,
it's whether you get up.

—Vince Lombardi

In the late 1950s, my father could have been the poster child for "The American Dream." He was 42 years old, had sold his textile business for millions, and was retired, living the good life with his wife and two kids in Beverly Hills. In order to keep himself busy, he invested in the stock market.

Brokers would call my father two, three, four times a day with their "investment" ideas. "Jack, Bethlehem Steel looks good, . . . Jack, I like the autos, . . . Jack, how about we buy Woolworth and put it away for 20 years?" After my father invested all his cash, the brokers introduced him to a new investment technique: margin. "Jack, we can buy twice the amount of companies by using the stocks in your portfolio as margin. You will make double the amount of money when the stocks go up. Remember, stocks always go up if you hold them long enough."

This made sense to my father and he went along with the strategy. In May 1962, my father went bankrupt. On the day my mother was being operated on for cancer, the brokers who told my father that stocks always go up if you hold them long enough were mass liquidating his portfolio to meet the margin calls. My family's net worth was not only wiped out, but we owed the brokerage houses money. This was my first experience with the *buy-and-hold* strategy that has once again become so popular with Wall Street.

My family packed a moving van and was forced to move back east. This was hard enough, but fate was not done with my father. Our moving van caught fire in Needles, Arizona, and all our possessions were destroyed.

There is an old saying that a dog will do one of two things if you kick him when he's down. The first is, he will roll over and die. The other is, he will not take it anymore and will jump up and bite you. The second analogy describes my father. Within five years, he had again created and again sold a multimillion dollar textile company. The Cooper family was able to sing, "California here we come, just back where we started from . . ."

This time, even though my father decided he was going to enjoy the country club life he was entitled to, there was a lingering matter that needed to be settled. He was going to make back the money he lost in the stock market!

With this goal in mind, my father knew he needed to create a method that wasn't a *buy-and-hold* strategy. After doing much research, he discovered that the most profitable game was to buy "hot" initial public offerings (IPOs) and secondaries and sell them for small gains. Within a few years, my father was not only the largest player on Wall Street in the IPO game, but he had earned back all the money he had lost in 1962. A couple of years later, he had his revenge and retired with many more millions than he started with. This is where I come in.

By the early 1980s, I had started and sold a small business and found myself gravitating toward Wall Street. After a brief six-month stint at Drexel Burnham, I went off on my own and attempted to replicate my father's success in the IPO market. Unfortunately for me, the rules had now changed. Mutual funds, not individuals, were the major beneficiaries of the brokerage house allotments for the deals, and I was given such a small amount of stock that I knew I could never make a decent living at it. I therefore decided to apply myself to studying the markets and, lo and behold, by 1987, I had become a big-picture, *buy-and-hold* investor. I can remember the calls from brokers. "Hey Jeff, Enzobiochem Information Systems Technologies is going to earn $0.30 this year, $2.00 next year, and $15.00 the year after. Even though the stock is at 100 times earnings today, it's at two times 1989's numbers! It's a steal!!!" And, as a rising tide lifts all ships, a rising bull market lifts all stocks. I was making great money until October 1987 when the *buy-and-hold* curse hit another member of the Cooper family. Fortunately, I did not go bankrupt, but I did get hurt and I learned a bitter lesson. Just as my father had twenty years earlier, I set out on a quest to create a methodology to beat the stock market.

It is now nine years later and I can confidently say that my quest has been successful. I make my living trading stocks and, more importantly, I do it from both the long side and the short side. If and when we go into a bear market, I know there will be no effect on my earnings and I will be one of the few players out there whose lifestyle will not change.

My strategies are simple and to the point. They revolve around price action and the notion that a stock in motion will remain in motion for at least the short term (a few minutes to a few days). My techniques are the culmination of 15 years of observation, testing, and most importantly, real-life results. Unlike what many other authors of investment books would have you believe about their strategies, my techniques are not perfect (not even close). They do, though, give me an edge, and this edge, combined with proper risk control, allows me to make a comfortable living.

Before we proceed to the chapters describing my trading strategies, we will look first at the background and rules you need to know to properly trade my methodology. I recommend you give special attention to chapter 4. This is the chapter that teaches you how to identify the proper stocks to trade, and I consider this to be the backbone of my success.

Finally, my goal in writing this manual is to teach you a handful of short-term, low-risk setup patterns. The patterns will allow you to avoid the disasters associated with *buy-and-hold* and will give you a set of tools to use to profit from the stock market for the rest of your life. After you have studied the manual, I hope you will find I achieved my mission.

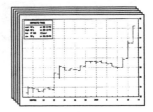

CHAPTER **2**

TERMS YOU NEED TO KNOW BEFORE STARTING

░ ░

I shall not mingle conjectures with certainties.

—Sir Isaac Newton

Before we go on to how I create my hit list and my trading strategies, I feel it would be best to review the definitions of the terms we will be using.

ADX—A mathematical formula used to measure the strength of a trend. A measurement of above 30 means the stock is trending strongly. Note that a *downtrend* will also create a high ADX number, just as will an up-trend. (See appendix for formula.)

Bar Chart—Shows the trading range (today's high minus today's low) of the day, its open, its high, its low, and its close. For example, if a stock opens at 65 and trades as low as 64 and as high as 66 and closes at 65 1/2, the bar would look like this:

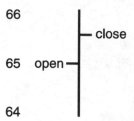

Bid—The highest price for a stock that buyers are willing to pay.

Breakdown—A stock that trades below a previously established low.

Breakout—A stock that trades above a previously established high.

+DI, –DI—A companion to ADX. As we just noted, ADX only measures the presence of a trend. +DI and –DI tell the direction of the trend. When a stock is trending higher, its +DI reading will be higher than its –DI reading and vice versa. (See appendix for formula.)

Gap—This means today's opening is above or below yesterday's high or low.

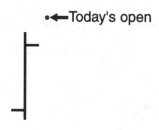

Inside Day—Today's high is equal to or less than the previous trading day's high, and today's low is equal to or greater than the previous trading day's low.

Price Persistency—One-way continuation of price. For example, a stock trades higher today, and again tomorrow, and again the next day, etc.

Relative Strength (as measured by *Investor's Business Daily*)—This tells the percentage of other stocks this stock has outperformed in price appreciation over the period of the last 12 months. The higher the number, the stronger the stock and vice versa.

Reversal—When a stock moves up and then changes direction and moves down (and vice versa).

Secondary Offering—When a public company sells additional stock to the public.

Moving Average—The average closing price of a stock over X number of days, i.e., a 10-day moving average is the average closing price of the previous 10 trading sessions.

Offer (also the "Ask")—The lowest price for a stock that sellers are willing to sell the stock for.

Stops—An order to buy or sell at the market if a stock trades at or through a specified price (stop price).

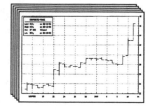

CHAPTER 3

RULES ARE MADE TO BE BROKEN—EXCEPT THESE

▪ ▪

*I base my calculation on the expectation
that luck will be against me.*

—Napoleon

1. Money management is more important than entry strategies. This means keeping losses to a minimum. In my opinion (and unfortunately, experience) 98 percent of all large losses were originally small losses. This fact must be ingrained into your psyche! Controlled position size combined with stop-loss management increases returns while decreasing risk.

2. *The trend rules!* About 90 percent of the time, I trade in the direction of a strongly trending market. This is identified by ADX, Relative Strength, New Highs/New Lows, and Moving Averages (see chapter 4).

3. Sponsorship is critical. I do not have the patience to wait for Wall Street to discover the next Microsoft. I trade in the stocks that the momentum growth funds are in. Louis Navellier's *MPT Review* newsletter and *Investor's Business Daily* each do superior jobs of identifying which

stocks are gaining sponsorship (participation in a stock by major players) and which stocks are losing sponsorship (more on this in chapter 4).

4. I start everyday at zero. This means I will eliminate immediately any and all positions not moving in my favor. This reduces my overall risk and allows me to protect my profits.

5. Never forget: The longer a position is held, the more things can go wrong.

6. Because of the high turnover of trading, commission costs must be kept to a minimum. You will have a difficult time maximizing your profits if you trade for more than 6¢/share.

7. Most stockbrokers are good people. Unfortunately, most (not all) do not have a clue. I therefore make all of my own decisions.

8. Trading is a serious business! If you were to open a retail store you would need a cash register, phones, etc. The same is true for trading. I recommend you get the best data feed, hardware, trading software program, etc., you can afford. Remember, you are competing against hundreds of brokerage houses and thousands of traders who have state-of-the-art equipment.

9. Overall, stock market direction is fun to ponder, but beyond a few days it is impossible to predict. My strategies are based on short-term factors, not macroeconomic views.

10. Most of my trading decisions are made by relying on technical analysis and pattern recognition. Fundamental factors, though considered, are not as important as technical factors.

11. I prepare for the day, as much as possible, the evening before. There is too much chaos in the morning to properly get ready for the day.

12. I became a much more profitable trader when I learned to scratch a trade. This means breaking even, losing an eighth or a quarter, etc. I have learned to put my ego in check and realize I am usually right approximately 60 percent of the time. If I can minimize my losses when I am wrong I am assured of remaining a profitable trader.

13. *Doubling-up is for losers!* When a trade moves against me I look to get out of it, not add to it! I know an individual trader who kept adding to his Micron Technologies position as it dropped from 85 to 20! It will be

years before he ever possibly *breaks even*. Thank you, but no thank you. Again—when a position moves against you—*get out!*

14. I lighten my positions and lessen my trading before news events (major economic news, earnings, etc.). Too many traders get killed when they make a "bet" on the report and are wrong. If you need to gamble, go to Vegas. At least there you get "comped" for losing!

15. This is not an easy game, especially when a major market move (like the bull market which began in 1982) ends. **There are probably fewer *full-time* professional traders in this country than there are professional athletes.** You must be prepared to work as hard and to be as persistent as a professional athlete to become truly successful.

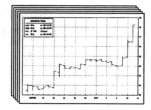

CHAPTER 4

CREATING THE HIT LIST

• •

Out of clutter find simplicity; from discord make harmony.

—Albert Einstein

This is the most important chapter in the book. I firmly believe my methodology works because of the stocks I trade in. Therefore, creating and constantly modifying my list is a critical, on-going process.

For me to make a consistent living at this game, I must be in stocks that are trending strongly. This allows me the opportunity of being in the "right" stocks nearly everyday. It is next to impossible to make a living by trading stocks that are moving sideways! I also tend to trade in higher-priced stocks. It is a lot easier for a $60 stock to move four points and trade to $64 than it is for a $12 stock to trade to $16. Finally, I ideally want to trade in fairly illiquid stocks that are under accumulation or distribution. This creates higher volatility, hence greater opportunity for profits.

I create my hit list every Sunday, and adjust it each evening. One of the purposes of my list is to allow me to focus on a small handful of stocks (15–25 names) and not be distracted by the many things that are occurring to thousands of stocks daily. Even though there is some discretion involved in creating this list, the following criteria allow me to identify what I consider to be the most opportunistic stocks each day.

When you finish reading the trading strategies section, please refer to the appendix. There, I give further insight to help you create the daily list.

There are two main criteria and two minor criteria I use to identify the best names. The main criteria are trend and price, and the minor criteria are sponsorship and liquidity.

MAIN CRITERIA

1. **Trend**

   A. **ADX**—As I mentioned in chapter 2, ADX measures the strength of a trend. This is the single best indicator available to traders, yet it is the least used indicator. I highly recommend that you either buy a software package that has ADX, or program it yourself from the formula in the appendix. It will be worth your effort many times over.

      I usually want to trade only in stocks whose 14-period ADX is greater than 30 (the higher, the better). A reading of above 30 tells me the overall trend for this stock is strong. In rising markets it signals accumulation, and in declining markets it means there is persistent distribution. For uptrending stocks, the +DI reading must be greater than the –DI reading, and vice versa for declining stocks. Therefore, Rule #1 is: Trade stocks whose ADX is greater than 30.

      - OR -

   B. **Relative Strength (RS),** as measured by *Investor's Business Daily*—If you are unable to use ADX, only trade stocks whose RS is 95 or higher.

      Relative strength is a terrific measurement offered by *Investor's Business Daily*. William O'Neil has done a phenomenal job with his newspaper by offering investors and traders a chance to identify the best performing stocks. My only criticism of RS is that it will not allow you to create a short-selling list (especially pertinent in bear markets). Unfortunately, extremely low RS readings usually are associated with stocks that are trading for $2 or $3 a share, and I don't trade those.

One way to possibly create a short list is to look at those stocks whose RS has recently dropped below 30. *Investor's Business Daily* has that list and it may be of help. In the meantime Rule #2 is: RS must be 95 or above for uptrending stocks if ADX is not being used. RS should recently have broken under 30 for short selling candidates.

C. **Moving Averages**—A few of my strategies require the use of moving averages. For these strategies, the long candidates must be trading above both their 10-day and 50-day moving averages and the short candidates must be trading below their 10-day and 50-day moving averages.

D. **New Highs/New Lows**—A small handful of my strategies only require a stock to make either a two-month new high or a two-month new low. My computer identifies this list for me on a nightly basis and I then filter the list with price, average daily volume, and sponsorship.

2. **Price**—As I mentioned earlier, I prefer to trade in higher-priced stocks. For a $10 stock to move three points requires a 30 percent move. For a $50 stock to move three points requires a 6 percent move. This may seem like common sense but most traders flock to low-priced stocks and avoid the higher-priced stocks like the plague. Therefore, Rule #3 is: Only trade in stocks whose price is above $30 a share and preferably above $40 a share.

MINOR CRITERIA

3. **Sponsorship**—I want to buy stocks that are under accumulation by the major players and short stocks that are under distribution by these players. This sponsorship is what fuels the volatility in stocks. I identify these stocks with the help of Louis Navellier's *MPT Review* newsletter. Navellier has done a phenomenal job managing money by identifying which industries money is flowing into and out of. I highly recommend subscribing to his service (see the appendix for address information).

4. **Liquidity**—Even though I trade in all of the so-called momentum stocks, I have found the better moves occur in the less liquid stocks (average volume under 200,000 shares a day). Therefore, it is good to

trade Microsoft, Cisco Systems, and Nike, but it is even better to trade their less active counterparts.

Does a stock have to fit all of the preceding criteria to make my list? No! The criteria are simply a way for me to find a group of names that will allow me to maximize my strategies. As you will see from the hit list I used for the week of June 10, 1996 (see chapter 17), only a few of the names had all of the qualifications listed. **The common theme of this list is that they are all higher-priced trending stocks that have the ability to move quickly once a setup occurs.**

Again, in the appendix, I have gone into further detail on how to create the hit list. This should help further simplify the process for you. It will probably take you a while to get used to creating this weekly list but eventually it will become habit and you will then have the proper names to focus on each day.

PART ONE

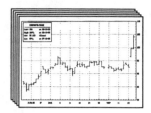

MAIN STRATEGIES

● ●

My main strategies reflect my five best strategies. If you told me I could only trade two or three of my strategies, I would choose them from this list. These are my bread-and-butter setups and allow me the luxury of being a professional trader. In baseball terms this would be a starting rotation of Sandy Koufax, Roger Clemens, Bob Gibson, Whitey Ford, and Nolan Ryan. With this type of lineup, I know that when one fails me I still have another four to bail me out and make me profitable.

A word of warning needs to be made before proceeding. The examples in this book were chosen for their educational value and most were successful trades. In the real world, unsuccessful trades are scattered in with the winners. The following examples do, though, show the type of profit potential the setups can lead to.

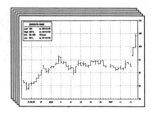

CHAPTER 5

EXPANSION BREAKOUTS™

■ ■

Fortune favors the bold.

—Caesar

I will begin the trading strategies section with two maxims:

1. You cannot buy every new high.

2. Not all breakouts are created equal.

It took me years and many thousands of dollars to realize this. In my early trading days, I mistakenly assumed that a new high was a new high and when it occurred, it must be bought. Only after finding myself on the wrong side of these breakouts when they reversed did I realize there had to be another piece to the strategy.

In studying the breakouts that most consistently led to one- to five-day profits, I noticed one common theme: the best breakouts were accompanied by a daily range that was the largest range of the previous nine trading sessions.

I then noticed (and this now applies to all my strategies) that the next day the stock had to trade above the Expansion Breakout day. This told me that the buying power from yesterday was continuing today.

Finally, I noticed that the trades that worked best tended to have very small intraday pullbacks, hence my stops should be tight to protect me if I am wrong.

With this said, let's look at the rules to trade Expansion Breakouts:

FOR BUYS

1. Today (day one) must be a two-month calendar high. (This strategy does not use ADX, nor RS. I simply want a new high accompanied by a range expansion).

2. Today's range (high minus low) must be equal to or larger than the largest daily range of the previous nine trading days.

3. Tomorrow only, buy 1/8 point above today's high.

4. Initial maximum risk (stop) is 1 point **under yesterday's close**.

FOR SHORT SALES
(HEREBY KNOWN AS EXPANSION BREAKDOWNS)

1. Today (day one) must be a two-month calendar low.

2. Today's range must be equal to or larger than the largest daily range of the previous nine trading days.

3. Tomorrow only, sell short 1/8 point under today's low.

4. Our initial protective stop is 1 point **above yesterday's close**.

Let's look at a handful of examples to help better understand this strategy.

EXAMPLE 5.1—Nike

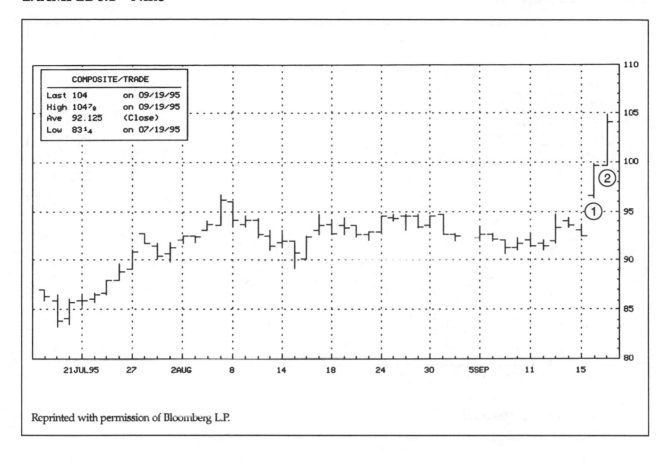

Reprinted with permission of Bloomberg L.P.

1. September 18, 1996—Nike makes a two-month high and its daily range is the largest range of the previous nine trading sessions. Tomorrow, if Nike trades 1/8 of a point above today's high of 99 3/4, we will go long.

2. Nike opens at 99 5/8 and trades up to 99 7/8, and we buy. Our initial protective sell stop is immediately placed 1 point under yesterday's close of 99 5/8. Yesterday's Expansion Breakout continues its upside move as the stock closes at 104, up 4 1/8 points from our entry point.

EXAMPLE 5.2—US Robotics

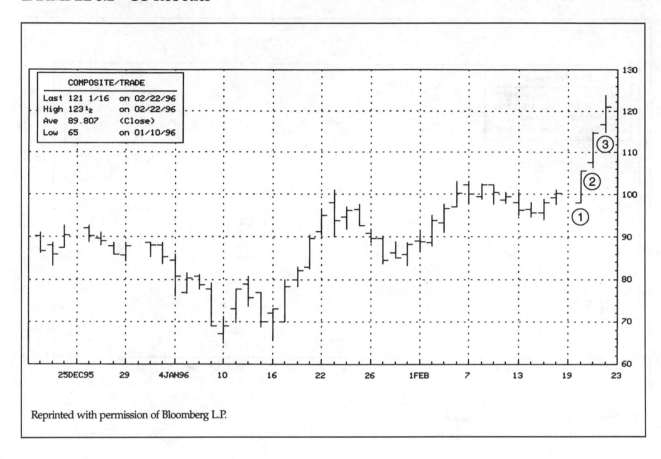

COMPOSITE/TRADE

Last	121 1/16	on 02/22/96
High	123½	on 02/22/96
Ave	89.807	(Close)
Low	65	on 01/10/96

Reprinted with permission of Bloomberg L.P.

1. February 20, 1996—US Robotics' daily range is the largest range of the previous nine days and makes a two-month new high.

2. The next morning, the stock gaps open above the previous day's high and we are long at 107 1/2. Our protective stop is placed at 104 3/4, 1 point under yesterday's close. After trading down to 106 1/2, the stock resumes its move, closing 7 1/4 points above our entry.

3. The rise continues the next day, taking US Robotics to as high as 123 1/2.

EXAMPLE 5.3—Citrix Systems

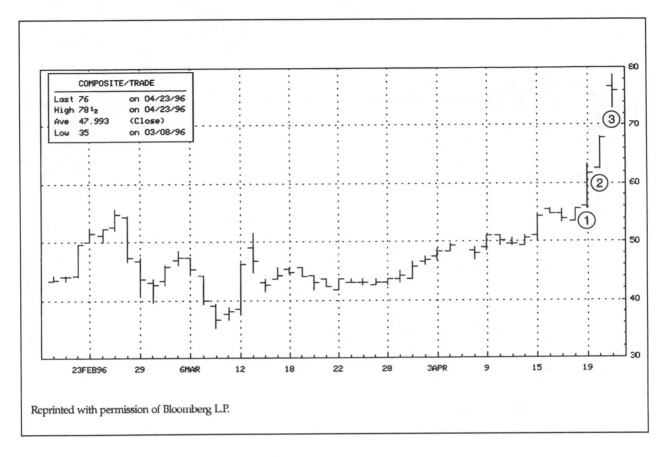

Reprinted with permission of Bloomberg L.P.

1. April 19, 1996—Citrix Systems has an Expansion Breakout.

2. The next day, the computer software server company trades 1/8 above* the previous day's high, and we are long at 63 3/8. Our sell stop is at 60 3/4, 1 point under yesterday's close.

3. Sometimes its better to be lucky than smart. The next morning the stock explodes to the upside, opening at 76 3/4, 13 3/8 points above our entry.

I should point out, it is exciting when this type of move occurs, but in reality, it is usually the exception, not the rule.

* *I will take a signal even if a stock gaps significantly.*

EXAMPLE 5.4—Shiva

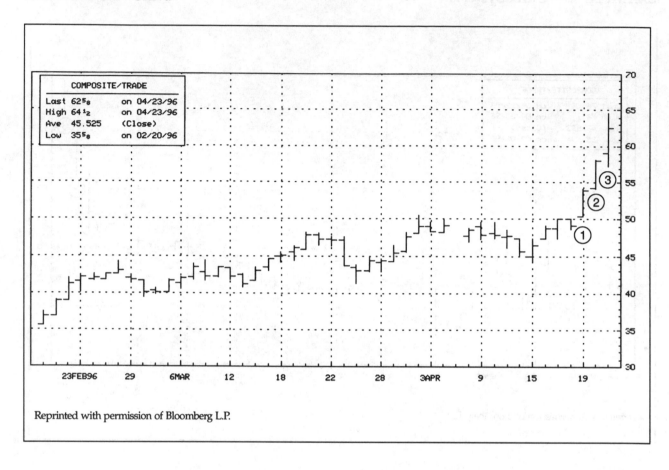

Reprinted with permission of Bloomberg L.P.

An interesting phenomenon I have profited from, and one to be aware of, is that of multiple stocks in an industry having Expansion Breakouts on the same day. This is a powerful signal and should be exploited when observed. As you can see from this example, Shiva (same industry as Citrix Systems) had an Expansion Breakout the same day as Citrix.

1. An Expansion Breakout.

2. Buy at 54 3/8 (open) and our stop is at 53.

3. Shiva trades to as high as 64 1/2 the following afternoon.

EXAMPLE 5.5—Oxford Health

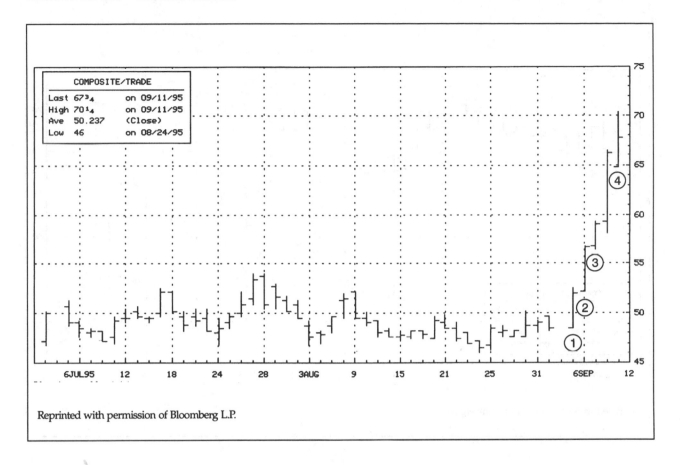

COMPOSITE/TRADE

Last	67³₄	on 09/11/95
High	70¹₄	on 09/11/95
Ave	50.237	(Close)
Low	46	on 08/24/95

Reprinted with permission of Bloomberg L.P.

1. Not an Expansion Breakout. Oxford does not make a two-month high.

2. An Expansion Breakout setup. A new high accompanied by the largest range of the previous nine sessions.

3. We buy 1/8 above yesterday's high of 56 3/4 and our initial protective stop is at 54 3/4.

4. The stock moves nearly 20 percent higher in a week.

EXAMPLE 5.6—Digital Equipment

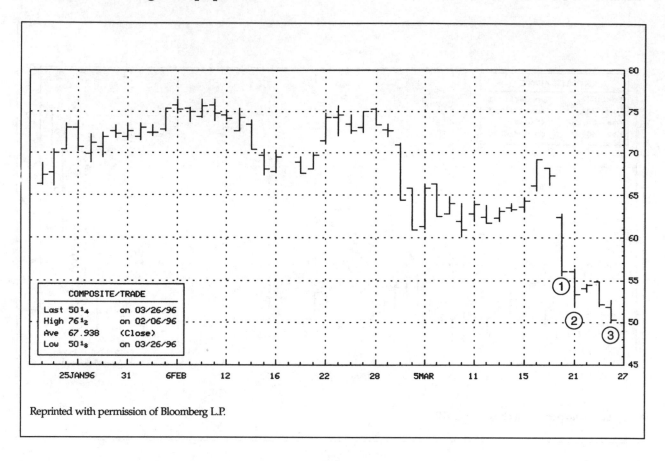

COMPOSITE/TRADE

Last	50 1/4	on 03/26/96
High	76 1/2	on 02/06/96
Ave	67.938	(Close)
Low	50 1/8	on 03/26/96

Reprinted with permission of Bloomberg L.P.

Even though I mostly trade this strategy from the long side, it works equally well to the downside.

1. An expansion breakdown.

2. Trades 1/8 under yesterday's low of 55 1/2. We sell short at 55 3/8 and our stop is at 57, 1 point above yesterday's close. The stock closes at 53 1/4.

3. Digital Equipment loses 10 percent of its value within four trading sessions.

EXAMPLE 5.7—Chiron

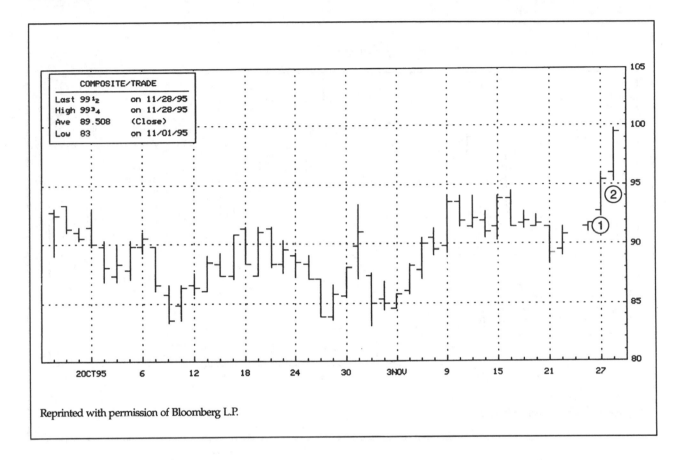

COMPOSITE/TRADE

Last	99½	on 11/28/95
High	99¾	on 11/28/95
Ave	89.508	(Close)
Low	83	on 11/01/95

Reprinted with permission of Bloomberg L.P.

1. Two-month new high and the largest range of the previous nine trading sessions.

2. Buy at 96 1/4, and Chiron closes 4 1/2 points above our entry.

EXAMPLE 5.8—Computer Horizons Corporation

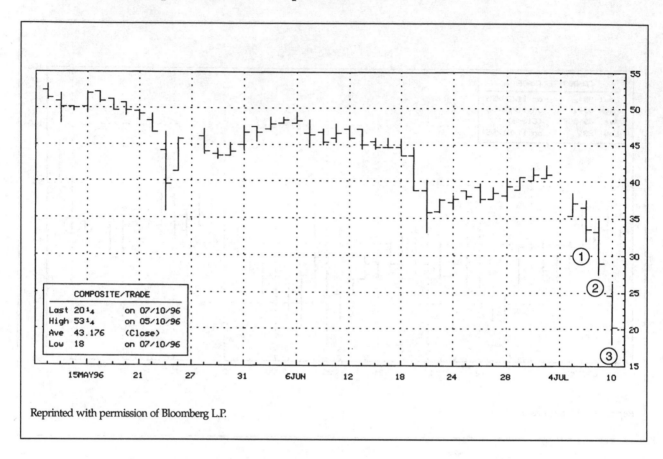

COMPOSITE/TRADE

Last 20¼   on 07/10/96
High 53¼   on 05/10/96
Ave   43.176 (Close)
Low   18   on 07/10/96

Reprinted with permission of Bloomberg L.P.

1. The largest range of 10 days and a two-month calendar low.

2. Sell short at 31 7/8.

3. The selling continues and Computer Horizons trades to as low as 18 within a day.

SUMMARY

Why do Expansion Breakouts work? I believe it is a combination of things. The first is that the trend (as measured by the new high or new low) is strong. The second is that large breakouts attract attention. Let's face reality. There are tens of thousands of momentum players on top of the billions of dollars in momentum-fund mutual funds looking to buy strength and sell weakness. A stock whose breakout is accompanied by a large range attracts attention. This setup begets buying, which attracts further buying. Also, many times this setup is accompanied by a significant news event: better earnings, a new product, a brokerage house recommendation—all bring new attention to the stock. Also, because we are many times trading in fairly illiquid stocks, it often becomes difficult for the institutions to accumulate the shares. They are therefore forced to pay up, causing prices to run even farther.

As traders, our job is not to look at the big picture. We are strictly looking for those setups that allow us to participate in short-term momentum moves, both long and short. Expansion Breakouts do exactly that. They do a terrific job of identifying those breakouts that are likely to experience significant follow-through.

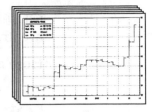

CHAPTER 6

1-2-3-4's

* *

I never did anything worth doing by accident,
nor did any of my inventions come by accident;
they came by work.

—Thomas Edison

One of the toughest predicaments for traders is deciding when to enter into runaway stocks. (Runaway stocks are those where the trend is *extremely* strong.) Most of us have gone through times where we identified a stock where we want to go long (or short) but, because the stock was moving so quickly, we never got a chance to enter.

The 1-2-3-4 trading strategy partially cures this problem. 1-2-3-4's were created by a friend of mine, Larry Connors. Larry is a full-time trader and is also the co-author of two excellent books on trading (see appendix).

In creating this strategy, Connors noticed how often strongly trending stocks would rest for three days before resuming their move. By waiting for this three-day pause, we can identify stocks that are catching their breath and can climb aboard before they race to new levels.

Here are the rules:

FOR BUYS

1. Identify a market whose 14-day ADX is greater than 30. *The higher the ADX, the better.* If you are not using ADX, the RS reading must be at 95 or higher.

2. The 14-day +DI reading must be greater than the 14 day −DI reading.

3. Wait for the market to have a 1-2-3 correction. This means that the market must have three consecutive lower lows or any combination of two lower lows and an inside day. The examples will clarify this further.

4. On day four only, buy 1/8 above the day-three high.

5. When filled, your initial protective stop should be near the day-three low.

6. As the position moves in your favor, you should trail your stops. In this setup, I tend to allow for a little more breathing room on my stops because of the upside potential of the moves.

FOR SHORT SALES

1. ADX must be greater than to 30. The higher the ADX, the better.

2. The –DI must be greater than the +DI.

3. Wait for a 1-2-3 rally. Three higher highs or any combination or two higher highs and an inside day.

4. On day four only, sell short 1/8 below the day-three low.

5. Your initial protective stop should be near the day-three high.

6. As the position moves in your favor, trail your stops.

EXAMPLE 6.1—Fila

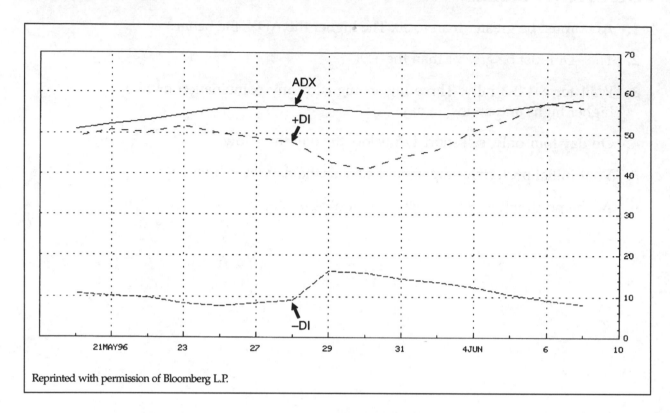

Reprinted with permission of Bloomberg L.P.

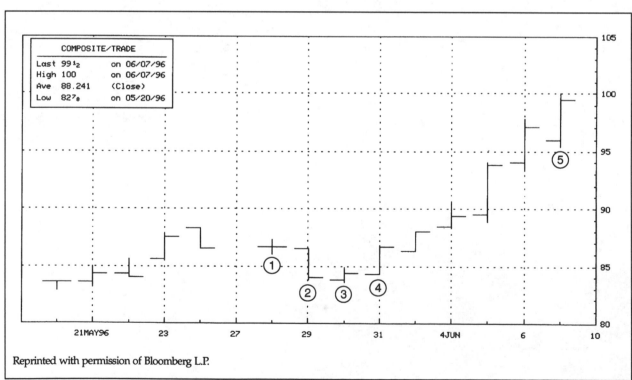

Reprinted with permission of Bloomberg L.P.

In late May, Fila is strongly trending higher. Its ADX reading is above 50 and its +DI reading is greater than its –DI reading.

1. A first lower low.

2. Second lower low.

3. Third consecutive lower low.

4. Buy at 85 1/8, one tick above the day-three high.

5. Fila's upward trend resumes and the stock trades nearly 15 points higher in six trading sessions.

EXAMPLE 6.2—Access Health

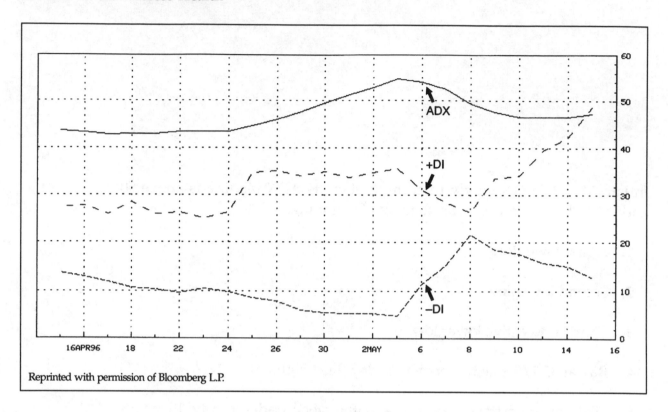

Reprinted with permission of Bloomberg L.P.

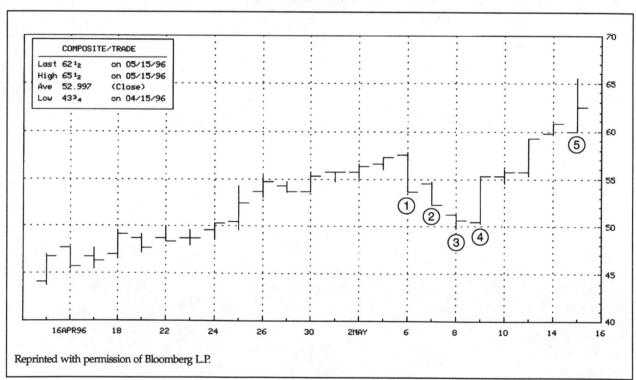

Reprinted with permission of Bloomberg L.P.

Access Health has a high ADX reading in an uptrending market.

1. First lower low.

2. Second lower low.

3. Third lower low.

4. Buy at 51 5/8, 1/8 above the day-three high, and our stop is at 49 3/4, the day-three low.

5. Access Health explodes more than 14 points above our buy entry.

EXAMPLE 6.3—Micron Technologies

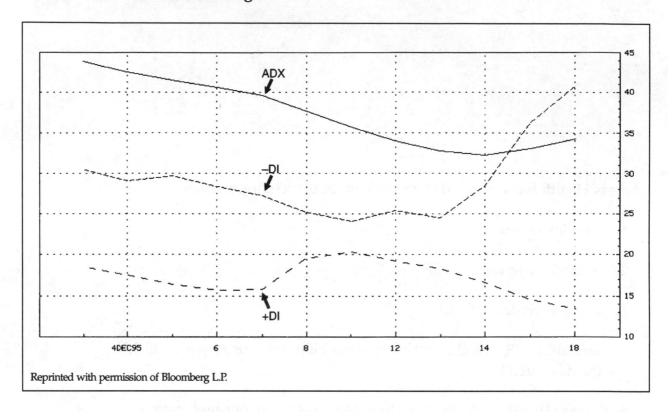

Reprinted with permission of Bloomberg L.P.

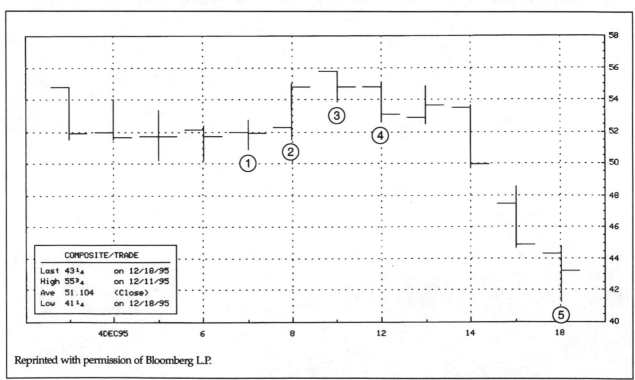

Reprinted with permission of Bloomberg L.P.

This strategy works equally well on the short side. Here is an example when the semiconductor stocks collapsed in 1995.

ADX is more than 30, the –DI is greater than the +DI = a bear trend.

1. First higher high.

2. Second higher high.

3. Third higher high.

4. Sell short at 53 3/4.

5. A 12-point profit in five trading days.

EXAMPLE 6.4—Luxottica Group

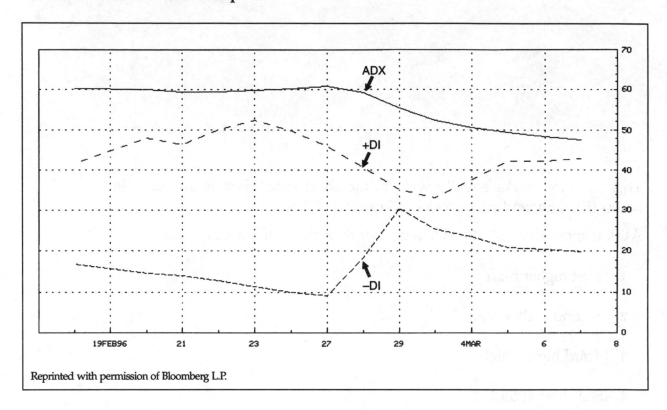

Reprinted with permission of Bloomberg L.P.

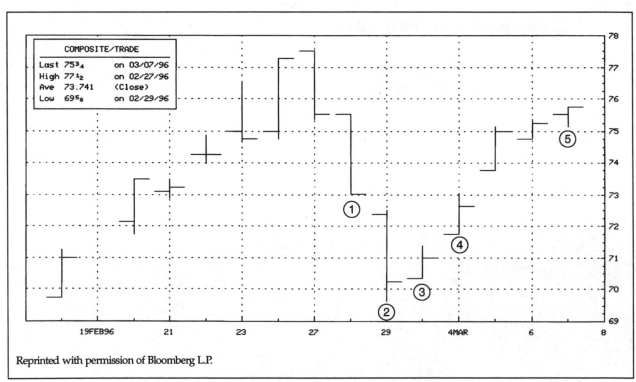

Reprinted with permission of Bloomberg L.P.

In late February 1996, Luxottica Group has an ADX reading above 30 and its +DI reading is greater than its –DI reading.

1. First lower low.

2. Second lower low

3. Inside day.

4. The stock opens above the previous day's high and, we are long at 71 3/4.

5. Luxottica trades 4 points higher in a few days.

EXAMPLE 6.5—NASDAQ 100 Index

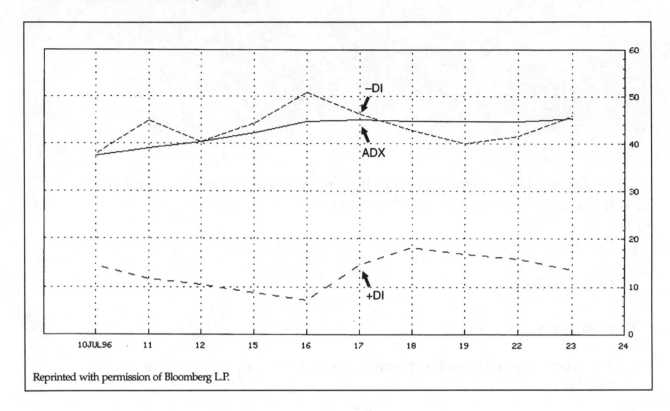

Reprinted with permission of Bloomberg L.P.

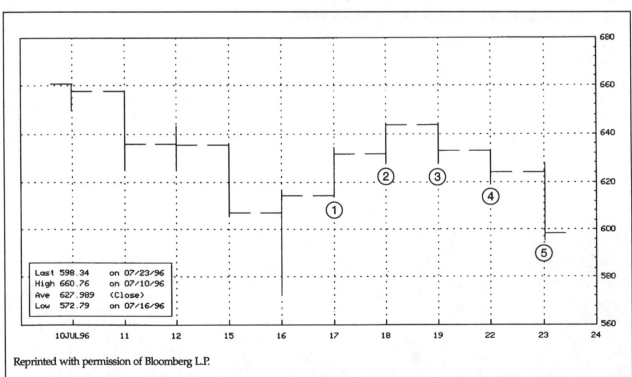

Reprinted with permission of Bloomberg L.P.

The NASDAQ suffered a serious sell-off in the summer of 1996. The ADX reading for the NASDAQ 100 Index was above 30, and the –DI was greater than the +DI.

1. First higher high.

2. Second higher high.

3. Inside day.

4. Sell signal triggered.

5. A 30-point loss within a day.

EXAMPLE 6.6—Netscape

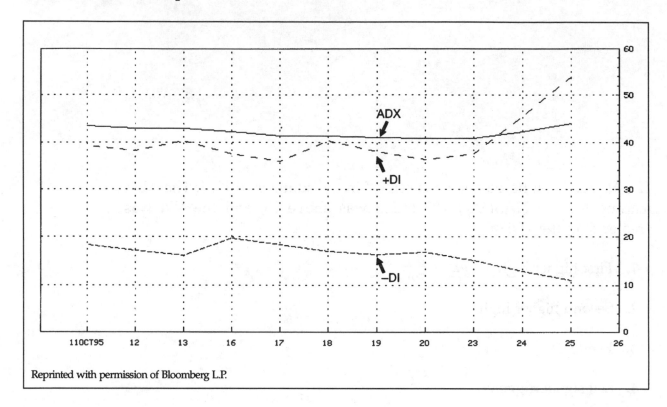

Reprinted with permission of Bloomberg L.P.

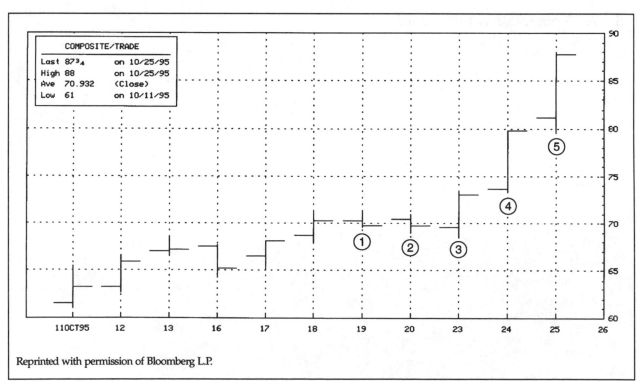

Reprinted with permission of Bloomberg L.P.

If you are looking for 1-2-3-4 setups to the upside, you can find them whenever a sector goes through a craze period. Here is an example in late 1995 from the Internet craze.

1. Inside day.

2. Lower low.

3. Lower low.

4. Buy at 73 3/4.

5. A 14 1/4-point profit in two days.

*** The stock hit 174 six weeks later!

SUMMARY

Of the five main strategies I trade, this setup occurs the least. This lack of opportunity, though, is compensated by the profit potential. Some of my biggest trades have come from this pattern, both on the long side and the short side.

Obviously, not every runaway market will experience three-day rests. Some rest only a day or two and others rest for four or five days. In spite of this, the most common resting period is three days, and that is usually the only variation I trade. As with most of the strategies, your initial risk is fairly small and, as you can see, the upside profit is substantial.

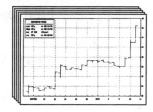

CHAPTER 7

STEPPING IN FRONT OF SIZE

● ●

The gods cannot help those who
don't seize opportunities.

—Confucius

Revealing this strategy is going to make every block trading-desk on Wall Street hate me.

Stepping in Front of Size on fairly thin NYSE and ASE stocks is a low-risk trick I use to make from 1/4 point to 4 points within a few minutes. What I do is I wait for a buyer to step in and show his hand on one of the stocks on my hit list. I then jump in front of him and take out the offer side of the market. This pushes prices a little higher, and if my new-found friend wants to get filled, he needs to pay a little more. Many times my buying causes other momentum buyers to buy, pushing prices higher, and eventually my friend gets impatient. He then tells the trading desk to "just buy the damn stock," pushing prices even higher and making me a little wealthier as I take my profits.

Here are the rules:

FOR BUYS

1. A stock must have an ADX reading of above 30 and its +DI greater than its –DI, or the stock must have an RS reading of 95 or higher.

2. The average daily volume for the stock should be under 200,000 shares a day. *The lower the volume, the more money you will make with this strategy.*

3. The stock *must* be trading higher for the day. This strategy doesn't work for stocks down on the day.

4. Most importantly, the buyer must show me he is impatient or I must see there is more than one institution trading this strategy. How do I know this? Because I am waiting for *two consecutive higher bid prices where there is size to buy.* ("Size" means 5,000 shares or more). For example, I want to see a market that has 5,000 shares bid at 52 and 1,000 offered at 52 1/4. I then want to see the bid go to 52 1/8 or 52 1/4 with 5,000 shares to buy again. This means someone is desperately looking for stock.

5. In the previous example, if the market goes to 52 1/8 bid (with 5,000 to buy) and 52 3/8 offer, I will pay the offer side. The only time I will ignore this higher bid is if I see 5,000 shares or more offered there. This means there may be a seller who can accommodate the large buyer.

6. My protective stop is 1/8 point under the price of the original 5,000 share bid (52).

7. Where I take profits is very subjective. Many times, if there is size on the offer side or if I see my new friend has been filled on his order, I will automatically take my profits.

Let's look at a few examples.

EXAMPLE 7.1—Flores & Rucks

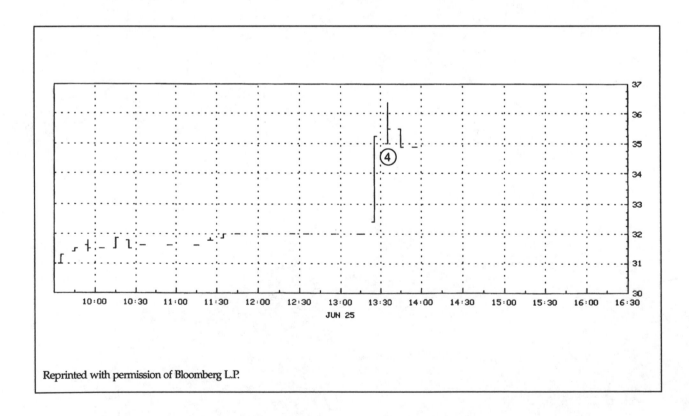

```
      Page                                          DG28 Equity Q R M
      Screen printed.
                     M A R K E T / T R A D E   R E C A P         Page 3
       Time    :     Min Vol      100    Volumes scaled by 100
       Date   6/25   Price Range          to
FLORES & RUCKS INC        (FNR    US)        PRICE 33¹₄    N    $
```

Time	E	Bid/Trd/Ask	E	Size	Cond	Time	E	Bid/Trd/Ask	E	Size	Cond
10:22	N	↓$31^1{}_2$		350	R2	10:16	N	$31^3{}_8$/$31^5{}_8$	N	50x10	①
10:22	N	$31^1{}_2$/$31^3{}_4$	N	10x10		10:11	N	$31^1{}_2$		1	
10:22	P	$31^1{}_2$/$31^3{}_4$	N	1x10		10:07	N	$31^1{}_2$		1	
10:22	B	$31^1{}_2$/$31^3{}_4$	N	1x10		10:07	N	$31^1{}_2$		1	
10:20	N	$31^5{}_8$/$31^7{}_8$	N	10x10		09:57	N	$31^1{}_2$		8	
10:20	N	↓$31^3{}_4$		150		09:54	N	↑$31^1{}_2$		15	
10:20	N	$31^3{}_4$/$31^7{}_8$	N	50x10		09:53	N	↓$31^3{}_8$		100	
10:20	N	$31^5{}_8$/$31^7{}_8$	N	50x10		09:53	N	$31^3{}_8$/$31^5{}_8$	N	10x10	
10:19	N	$31^3{}_4$/$31^7{}_8$	P	50x6		09:52	N	$31^3{}_8$/$31^5{}_8$	N	10x10	
10:19	N	$31^3{}_4$/$31^7{}_8$	P	50x6		09:52	N	↓$31^1{}_2$		100	
10:19	N	$31^7{}_8$		5		09:51	N	$31^1{}_2$/$31^3{}_4$	N	10x20	
10:19	N	↑$31^7{}_8$		5		09:50	N	$31^1{}_2$/$31^3{}_4$	N	10x4	
10:18	N	↑$31^3{}_4$		5		09:50	N	$31^3{}_4$		3	
10:18	N	$31^5{}_8$/$31^7{}_8$	N	50x10 ③		09:50	N	$31^1{}_2$/$31^3{}_4$	N	10x5	
10:18	N	↑$31^5{}_8$		5		09:50	N	$31^3{}_4$		5	
10:17	N	$31^1{}_2$/$31^3{}_4$	N	50x10		09:50	N	↑$31^3{}_4$		9	
10:17	N	$31^1{}_2$/$31^5{}_8$	N	50x10 ②		09:50	N	↑$31^5{}_8$		1	
10:17	N	$31^3{}_8$/$31^5{}_8$	N	150x10		09:50	N	$31^1{}_2$/$31^3{}_4$	N	10x20	

Reprinted with permission of Bloomberg L.P.

Flores & Rucks, an energy company, is a stock that not only had an ADX reading of 40, but was also on Navellier's list. (Sponsorship is always a plus.) Its average daily volume is less than 27,000 shares a day.

1. On June 25, 1996, with the stock trading higher for the day, a buyer shows 5,000 shares to buy at 10:16 A.M. A minute later, another buyer joins the fray and there are 15,000 shares to buy.

2. Immediately the bid gets raised to 31 1/2 with size, and our buy signal is triggered.

3. We buy at 31 7/8. Our protective stop is at 31 1/4, 1/8 under the original buyer's price.

4. The stock explodes more than 4 points before the buyers get filled.

EXAMPLE 7.2—Sun International Hotels

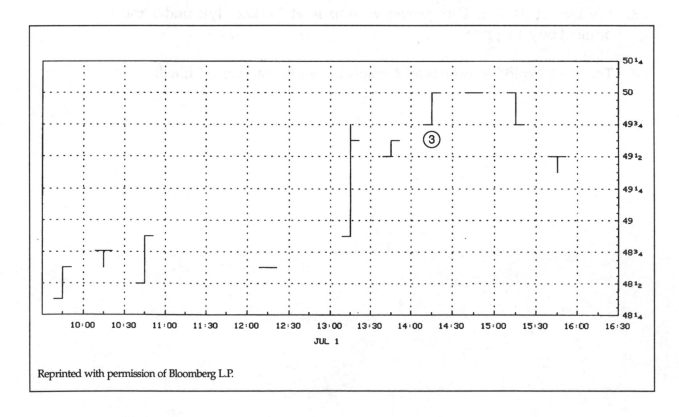

Page
Screen printed.

DG28 **Equity Q R M**

M A R K E T / T R A D E　R E C A P　　　　　Page 3
Volumes scaled by 100

Time ▨ : ▨　　Min Vol ▨ **100**
Date **7/1**　Price Range ▨▨▨ to ▨▨▨

SUN INTL HOTELS LTD　　(SIH　　US)　　　　PRICE 48　　N　　$

Time	E	Bid/Trd/Ask	E	Size	Cond	Time	E	Bid/Trd/Ask	E	Size	Cond
13:20	N	$49^3{}_8/49^3{}_4$	N	50x1		13:13	N	$49/49^1{}_8$	N	10x5	
13:20	N	$49^3{}_8/49^3{}_4$	B	50x1		13:13	N	$49/49^1{}_8$	N	5x5	
13:20	N	$\uparrow 49^5{}_8$		1		13:11	N	$48^3{}_4/49^1{}_8$	N	50x5	
13:19	N	$49^3{}_8/49^5{}_8$	N	50x1		13:00	N	$48^5{}_8/49$	N	50x5	②
13:18	N	$49^1{}_2$		10		13:00	N	$48^7{}_8$		5	
13:18	N	$49^1{}_2$		5		13:00	N	$\uparrow 48^7{}_8$		5	
13:17	N	$49^3{}_8/49^3{}_4$	N	50x5		12:38	N	$48^1{}_2/48^7{}_8$	N	50x5	①
13:17	N	$49^3{}_8/49^5{}_8$	B	50x1		12:24	N	$\downarrow 48^5{}_8$		34	
13:17	N	$49^1{}_2$		10		12:24	N	$48^1{}_2/48^7{}_8$	N	10x5	
13:17	N	$\uparrow 49^1{}_2$		5		10:54	N	$48^5{}_8/49$	N	20x5	
13:15	N	$49^1{}_4$		10		10:54	N	$48^1{}_2/49^1{}_8$	N	5x5	
13:15	N	$49^1{}_8/49^1{}_2$	N	50x5		10:54	N	$\uparrow 48^7{}_8$		11	
13:15	N	$\uparrow 49^1{}_4$		5		10:54	N	$48^1{}_2/49$	B	5x1	
13:14	N	$49/49^3{}_8$	N	50x5		10:41	N	$48^1{}_2/48^7{}_8$	N	5x5	
13:13	N	$49^1{}_8$		5		10:41	N	$\uparrow 48^3{}_4$		2	
13:14	N	$49/49^1{}_4$	B	50x1		10:39	N	$48^3{}_8/48^3{}_4$	N	5x5	
13:13	N	$49^1{}_8$		5		10:39	N	$\downarrow 48^1{}_2$		6	
13:13	N	$\uparrow 49^1{}_8$		5		10:29	N	$\uparrow 48^3{}_4$		1	

Reprinted with permission of Bloomberg L.P.

Reprinted with permission of Bloomberg L.P.

Sun International Hotels has an ADX reading greater than 30 and its trend is up, as measured by the +DI reading being greater than the –DI reading. Its average daily volume is approximately 66,000 shares a day.

1. At 12:38 P.M., 5,000 shares are bid at 48 1/2.

2. At 1:00 P.M., the buyer raises his bid to 48 5/8, triggering a buy signal.

3. The stock immediately explodes, taking the stock to as high as 50.

EXAMPLE 7.3—Sturm Ruger

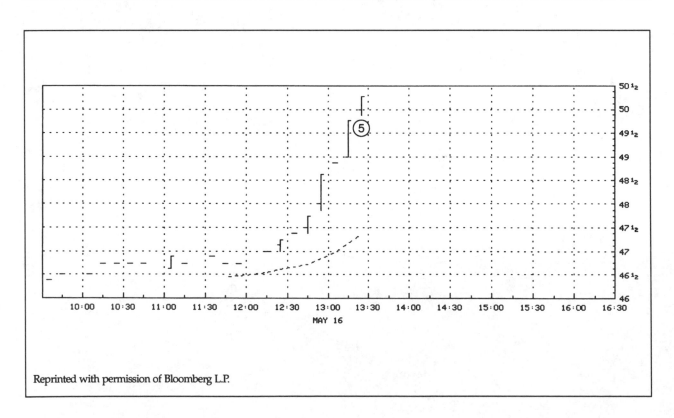


```
 Page                                                    DG26 Equity Q R M
 Screen printed.
                      M A R K E T / T R A D E   R E C A P                Page 3
       Time   :         Min Vol    100         Volumes scaled by 100
       Date  5/16   Price Range           to
 STURM RUGER & CO INC        (RGR    US)          PRICE 50      N    $
```

Time	E	Bid/Trd/Ask	E	Size	Cond	Time	E	Bid/Trd/Ask	E	Size	Cond
12:54	N	$48^1{}_2$		3		12:50	N	48		5	
12:54	N	$\downarrow 48^1{}_2$		3		12:50	N	$\uparrow 48$		5	
12:54	T	$\uparrow 48^5{}_8$		5		12:50	N	$47^3{}_4/48$	N	100x5	
12:54	N	$\uparrow 48^1{}_2$		6		12:50	N	$47^3{}_4/47^7{}_8$	T	100x5	OLDE
12:53	N	$48^1{}_4/48^1{}_2$	N	250x5 ④		12:50	N	$47^3{}_4/47^3{}_4$	T	100x5 ①	OLDE
12:53	N	$48^1{}_4$		5		12:49	N	$47^3{}_8/47^3{}_4$	T	5x5	OLDE
12:53	N	$48^1{}_8/48^1{}_2$	N	100x5		12:49	N	$\uparrow 47^3{}_4$		5	
12:53	N	$48^1{}_8/48^1{}_2$	T	100x5	OLDE	12:48	M	$\downarrow 47^3{}_8$		1	
12:53	N	$48^1{}_8/48^1{}_4$	X	100x1 ③		12:46	M	$47^1{}_2$		2	
12:53	N	$48^1{}_4$		5		12:46	N	$47^3{}_8/47^3{}_4$	T	5x5	OLDE
12:53	N	$48^1{}_4$		5		12:46	N	$47^3{}_8/47^1{}_2$	X	5x1	
12:52	N	$\uparrow 48^1{}_4$		12		12:46	M	$47^1{}_2$		8	
12:50	N	$48/48^1{}_4$	N	250x5		12:46	M	$47^3{}_8/47^1{}_2$	X	8x1	
12:50	N	$48/48^1{}_4$	T	250x5	OLDE	12:46	N	$47^1{}_2$		10	
12:50	N	$48/48^1{}_8$	P	250x1		12:46	M	$47^1{}_2$		8	
12:50	M	$\downarrow 47^7{}_8$		1		12:46	N	$47^1{}_2$		10	
12:50	N	$48/48$	X	250x1 ②		12:46	N	$\uparrow 47^1{}_2$		4	
12:50	N	48		5		12:34	M	$47^3{}_8/47^1{}_2$	N	8x5	

Reprinted with permission of Bloomberg L.P.

MAY 16

Reprinted with permission of Bloomberg L.P.

The gun company Sturm Ruger experienced a very strong upside move in the spring of 1996. This is just one example of many where institutions were tripping over each other in an effort to buy stock.

1. At 12:50 P.M., a buyer bids 10,000 shares at 47 3/4.

2. A few seconds later, the bid is raised (probably by a different buyer) to 48, triggering our buy signal.

3. Again, the bid gets raised.

4. Isn't this game fun?

5. The stock trades up to 50 1/4 before our dueling buyers get filled.

EXAMPLE 7.4—Chesapeake Energy Corp.

Page
Screen printed.

DG28 **Equity Q R M**

M A R K E T / T R A D E   R E C A P

Volumes scaled by 100

Page 13

Time ▮:▮ Min Vol 100

Date 6/21 Price Range ▮▮▮▮ to ▮▮▮▮

CHESAPEAKE ENERGY CORP   (CHK   US)   PRICE $80\tfrac{1}{2}$ N $

Time	E	Bid/Trd/Ask	E	Size	Cond	Time	E	Bid/Trd/Ask	E	Size	Cond
09:45	P	$76^7{}_8$/$77^1{}_8$	N	1x30		09:36	N	↑77		8	
09:45	M	$76^7{}_8$/$77^1{}_8$	N	1x30		09:36	N	$76^5{}_8$/77	N	50x5	②
09:45	N	↓77		1		09:36	N	$76^3{}_4$		3	
09:44	N	77/$77^1{}_8$	N	1x30		09:36	N	$76^3{}_4$		2	
09:43	N	$76^7{}_8$/$77^1{}_8$	N	5x20		09:35	N	$76^1{}_2$/$76^7{}_8$	N	50x5	
09:42	T	$77^1{}_8$		1		09:35	N	↑$76^3{}_4$		7	
09:40	N	$76^7{}_8$/$77^1{}_8$	N	5x5		09:34	P	$76^5{}_8$		1	
09:39	N	$76^7{}_8$/$77^1{}_4$	N	5x5		09:33	N	$76^1{}_2$/$76^3{}_4$	N	50x10	①
09:39	N	$77^1{}_8$		2		09:33	N	$76^1{}_2$/$76^3{}_4$	N	10x10	
09:38	T	$77^1{}_8$		4		09:33	N	$76^5{}_8$		1	
09:38	T	$77^1{}_8$		5		09:33	P	$76^5{}_8$		2	
09:37	N	$76^7{}_8$/$77^1{}_8$	N	5x5		09:33	M	$76^5{}_8$		1	
09:37	N	↑$77^1{}_8$		5		09:33	M	$76^5{}_8$		1	
09:37	N	$76^3{}_4$/$77^1{}_8$	N	2x5		09:33	N	↑$76^5{}_8$		19	
09:37	N	77		3							
09:37	N	77		3							
09:36	N	77		2							
09:36	N	$76^3{}_4$/77	N	2x5							

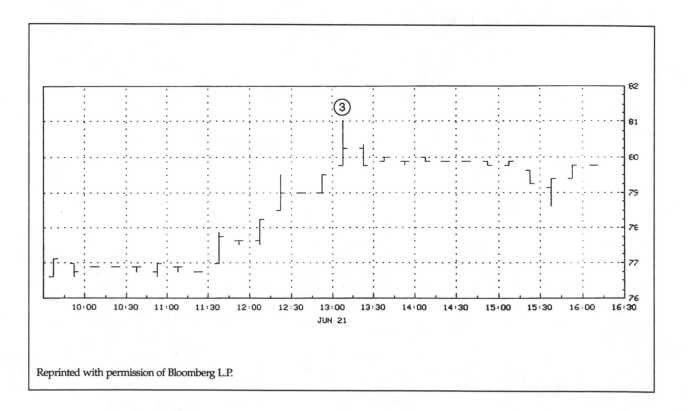

Chesapeake Energy Corp.

1. 5,000-share bid at 76 1/2.

2. Three minutes later the bid for 5,000 goes to 76 5/8, triggering our signal.

3. The chart shows how the stock explodes to above 81 before everyone gets filled.

SUMMARY

Why does this strategy work? I believe it's a combination of factors:

1. We are trading in fairly illiquid stocks. Large buyers have trouble accumulating these stocks.

2. We are trading stocks that are trending strongly. Uptrending stocks attract momentum buyers who push stocks higher, which attracts more buyers.

By Stepping in Front of Size, I also have a cushion to protect me in case prices reverse. Here is one problem with this strategy, though. Most times it is next to impossible to buy more than a few thousand shares before the stock heads higher. Therefore, if you are used to trading more size than this, the strategy is not appropriate for you. For the majority of short-term individual traders, though, this strategy is a bonanza.

The question you may ask now is, how about trading this on the short side with weak stocks? The answer is yes, it works to the downside also, except it comes with one problem—you need an uptick. If the seller(s) is(are) aggressive enough in his(their) pursuit to unload stock you may not get an uptick until he(they) is(are) done selling. Your discretion is needed, but the strategy is absolutely applicable to downtrending stocks.

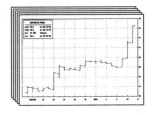

CHAPTER 8

EXPANSION PIVOTS™

■ ■

Fortune is always on the side of the largest battalions.

—Marquis de Sèvingnè

Expansion Pivots are another of the daily range expansion strategies I use to identify when institutions are piling into or bailing out of a stock.

Over the years, I have observed the number of times a stock will trade around its 50-day moving average for a period of time, and then without warning, explode either to the upside or downside. This explosion then follows through for at least a few days, giving traders like myself the opportunity to profitably participate in these moves.

Why is the 50-day moving average so significant? It is because institutions and traders use it as a benchmark indicator. This means that when a stock has a significant move off this level, it comes to the attention of literally thousands of money managers and traders. This group then jumps into or out of the stock as it moves away from the moving average. As you will see in some of the examples, the moves off the 50-day average can be significant.

Here are the rules:

FOR BUYS

1. Today's range is greater than the daily range of the past nine trading sessions.

2. Either yesterday or today the stock is trading at or below the 50-day moving average and explodes higher.

3. Tomorrow, buy 1/8 above the explosion-day high.

4. Our initial protective stop is 1 point **below the explosion day's close**.

FOR SHORT SALES

1. Today's range is greater than the daily range of the past nine trading sessions.

2. Either yesterday or today the stock is trading at or above the 50-day moving average and explodes lower.

3. Tomorrow, sell short 1/8 below the explosion-day low.

4. Our initial protective stop is 1 point **above the explosion day's close**.

EXAMPLE 8.1—IBM

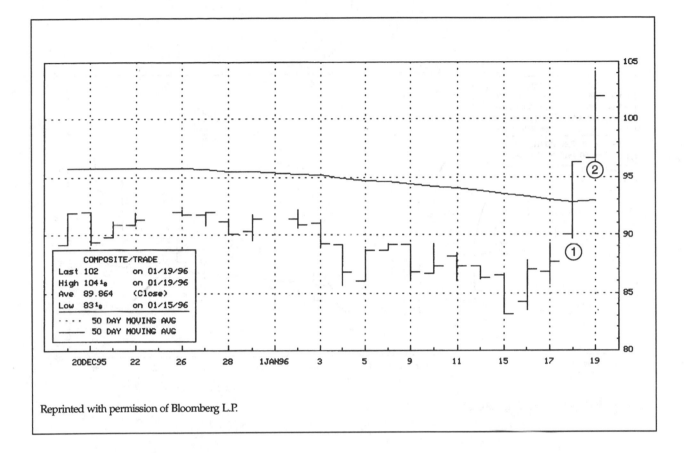

COMPOSITE/TRADE
Last 102	on 01/19/96
High 104⅛	on 01/19/96
Ave 89.864	(Close)
Low 83⅛	on 01/15/96

· · · · 50 DAY MOVING AVG
——— 50 DAY MOVING AVG

Reprinted with permission of Bloomberg L.P.

1. January 18, 1995—IBM trades through its 50-day moving average and its daily range is larger than the daily range of the previous nine trading sessions. If tomorrow trades 1/8 above today's high of 96 1/4, we will buy and our initial sell stop will be at 95 1/4, 1 point below today's close.

2. IBM opens at 96 5/8 triggering a buy signal and we are long. As you can see, the low of the day is 96 1/2, and we close 5 3/8 points higher than the entry.

An added point should be mentioned. Many times this setup leads to substantial intermediate term moves. In this example IBM traded up to 128 7/8 over the next five weeks.

EXAMPLE 8.2—Newbridge Networks

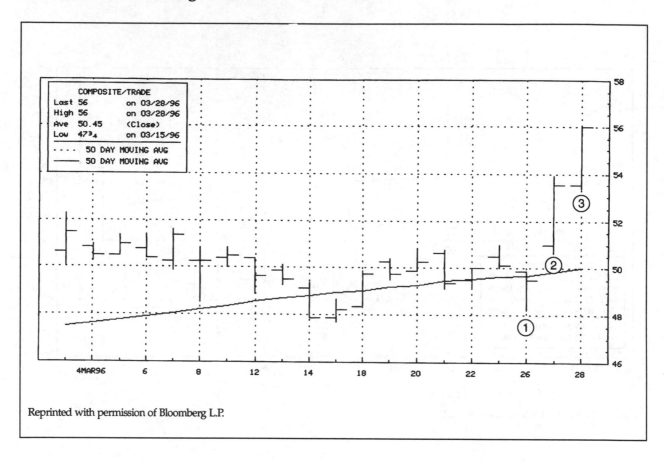

1. Newbridge Networks trades at its 50-day moving average.

2. The next day the stock explodes higher and has its largest range of 10 trading days.

3. We buy 1/8 above the previous day's high and the stock closes 2 points above our entry point.

EXAMPLE 8.3—Security Dynamics Technologies

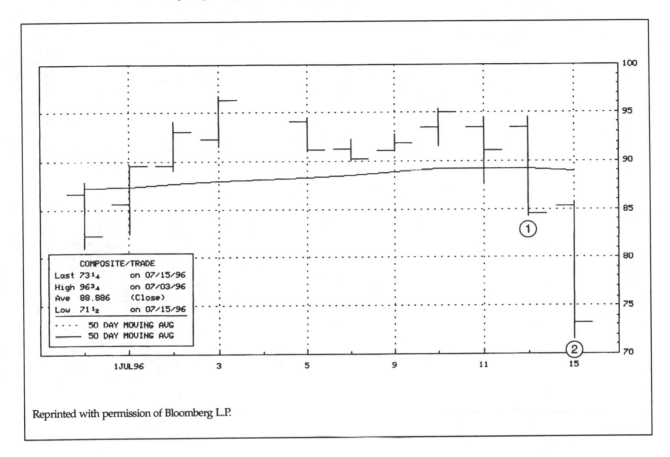

COMPOSITE/TRADE
Last 73¹₄   on 07/15/96
High 96³₄   on 07/03/96
Ave 88.886   (Close)
Low 71¹₂   on 07/15/96

· · · · 50 DAY MOVING AVG
——— 50 DAY MOVING AVG

1JUL96   3   5   9   11   15

1. Security Dynamics Technologies trades through its 50-day moving average and has a 10-day range expansion.

2. We sell short at 84 1/2, 1/8 under yesterday's low, and the institutions bail out, collapsing the stock more than 11 points intraday.

EXAMPLE 8.4—Fila

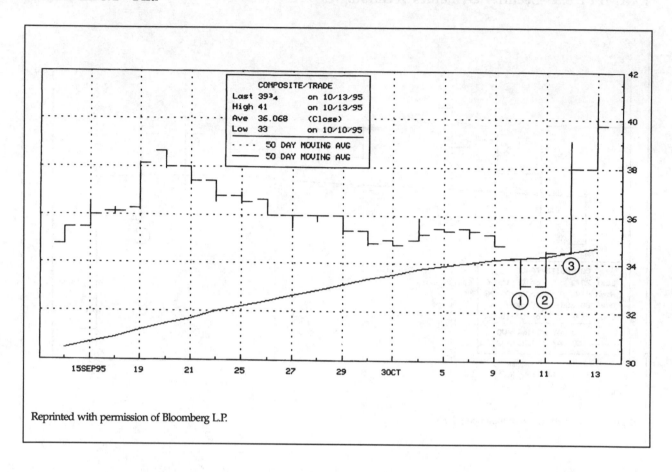

Reprinted with permission of Bloomberg L.P.

Here's an example of a setup which could have gone either way.

1. An expansion range off the 50-day moving average.

2. We will sell short to the downside if it trades under 33. In fact the stock reverses to the upside, trades through its 50-day moving average, and has the largest range of 10 days.

3. Buy at 34 5/8 and the stock closes at 38.

EXAMPLE 8.5—Schlumberger

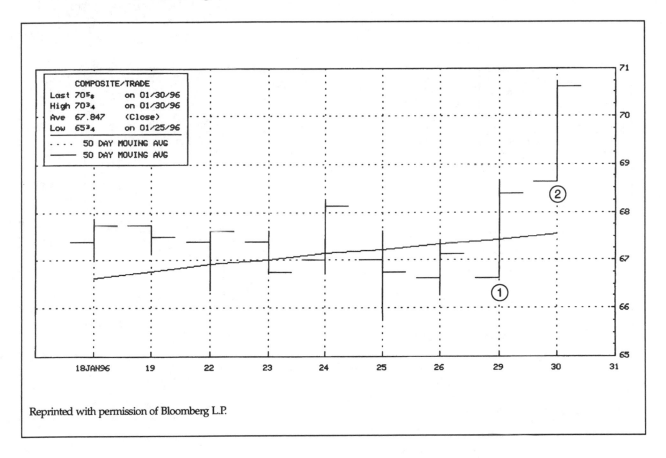

Reprinted with permission of Bloomberg L.P.

1. Schlumberger trades through its 50-day moving average and has a 10-day range expansion.

2. We buy at 68 3/4, and it trades as high as 70 3/4 intraday.

EXAMPLE 8.6—Zenith Electronics

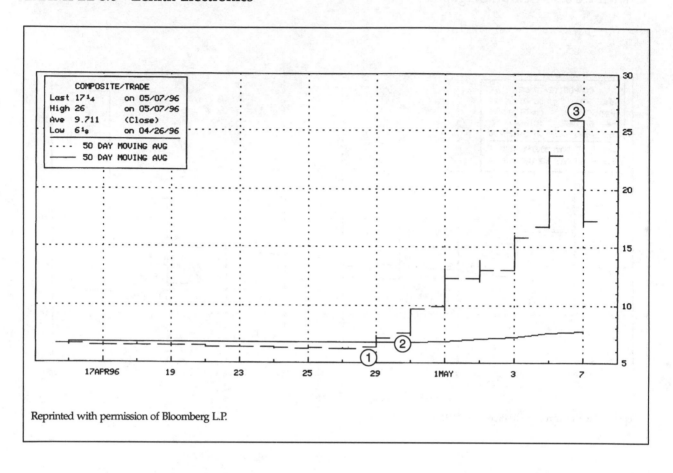

COMPOSITE/TRADE
Last 17¼   on 05/07/96
High 26   on 05/07/96
Ave 9.711   (Close)
Low 6⅛   on 04/26/96
- - - - 50 DAY MOVING AVG
———— 50 DAY MOVING AVG

Reprinted with permission of Bloomberg L.P.

Even though this is a low-priced example, it reflects the potential impact of this strategy.

1. Zenith trades through its 50-day moving average with the largest range of 10 days. It is also an Expansion Breakout, making the setup even stronger (see Putting Pieces Together, chapter 16).

2. Buy at 7 1/2 and it closes at 9 5/8.

3. Stock trades over 200 percent higher over the next week. (No, I didn't take this trade!)

SUMMARY

Expansion Pivots exploit the herd mentality on Wall Street. With so many players keying off the 50-day moving average, any significant movement off this average has these individuals piling into or out of a stock all at the same time. This creates one-way momentum, and I want to be part of that momentum. As you saw with a couple of the examples, sometimes this momentum leads to longer-term moves, but this does not interest me. I am strictly using this strategy as one that provides a short-term path of least resistance, and with so many players simultaneously buying or selling a stock, that path is usually unobstructed.

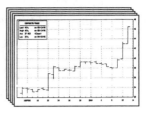

CHAPTER 9

180's™

....

When opposites supplement each other,
everything is harmonious.

—Lao Tsu

"180's" is a strategy I use to identify stocks that have a one-day trend reversal and then resume the trend. Simply stated, it is a two-day reversal pattern in the direction of the trend. This setup is one of the easier patterns to identify, and with a little practice it will begin to jump out at you.

As I have mentioned, I tend to trade stocks in the direction of the stock's trend. I am constantly looking for strong stocks that are pausing, and I wait to climb aboard as their move begins (up or down) again. 180's is the perfect strategy for this. In an uptrend, this setup waits for strongly trending stocks to close in the bottom of their range one day and close in the top of their range the following day.

Here are the rules:

FOR BUYS

1. On day one, the stock must close in the bottom 25 percent of its daily range. On day two, the stock must close in the top 25 percent of its range.

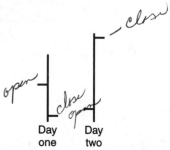

2. The stock's price must close greater than both its 10-day and its 50-day moving average on day two only. (Neither ADX nor RS are needed here since the trend is indicated by price relative to the moving averages).

3. Day three only, buy 1/8 point above the day-two high.

4. Our initial protective stop is 1 point **under our entry**.

FOR SHORT SALES

1. On day one it must close in the top 25 percent of its range. On day two, it must close in the bottom 25 percent of its range.

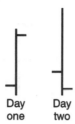

Day
one

Day
two

2. The stock's price must close under both its 10-day and its 50-day moving average on day two only.

3. On day three only, sell short 1/8 point under the day-two low.

4. Our initial protective buy stop is 1 point **above our entry**.

Let's look at six examples.

EXAMPLE 9.1—Microsoft

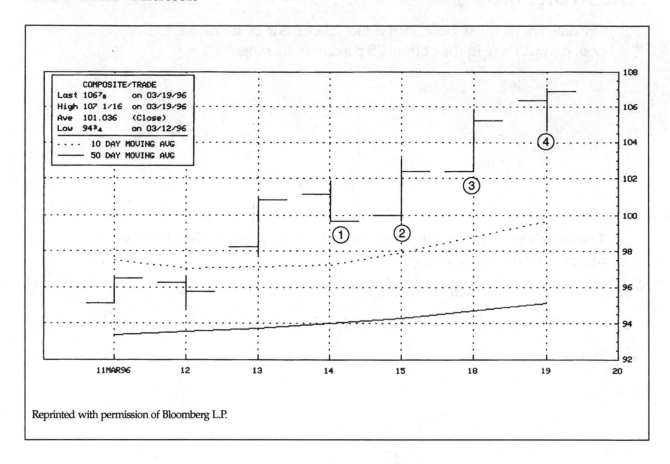

Reprinted with permission of Bloomberg L.P.

1. Microsoft closes in the bottom 25 percent of its daily range.

2. The next day, it closes in the top 25 percent of its range and above both its 10-day and 50-day moving averages.

3. We buy 1/8 above yesterday's high of 103 1/8, and our stop is at 102 1/4.

4. Microsoft trades 3 3/4 points above our entry.

EXAMPLE 9.2—Potash

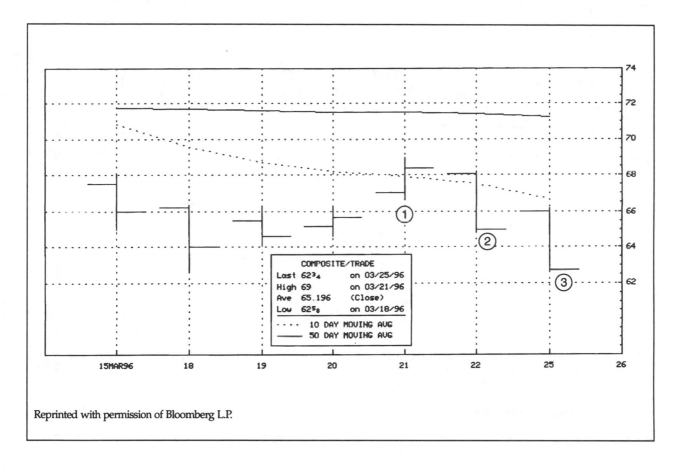

Reprinted with permission of Bloomberg L.P.

I especially like trading this stock. The specialist tends to get out of the way when size comes in, and it creates good volatility and opportunity.

1. Stock closes exactly in the top 25 percent of its range.

2. Potash closes in the bottom 25 percent of its range and under its 10-day and 50-day moving averages.

3. Our sell short signal is triggered at 64 5/8, 1/8 under the previous day's low. Our stop is at 65 5/8. (Even though this chart doesn't show it, the stock never touched its protective buy stop after we went short.) Potash closes at 62 3/4 for a 1 7/8-point profit.

EXAMPLE 9.3—Cabletron Systems

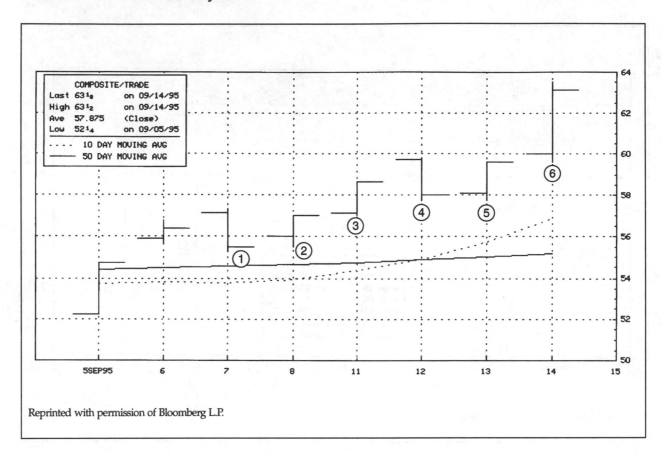

COMPOSITE/TRADE
Last 63 ⅛   on 09/14/95
High 63 ½   on 09/14/95
Ave 57.875 (Close)
Low 52 ¼   on 09/05/95
···· 10 DAY MOVING AVG
──── 50 DAY MOVING AVG

Reprinted with permission of Bloomberg L.P.

Here are two profitable trades in Cabletron Systems over a six-day period.

1. Closes in the bottom 25 percent of its range.

2. Closes in the top 25 percent of its range and above its 10-day and 50-day moving averages.

3. Buy at 57 1/8 (open), and it closes at 58 5/8.

4. Closes in the bottom 25 percent.

5. Closes in the top 25 percent and above its 10-day and 50-day moving averages.

6. Buy at 60, and it closes at 63 1/8, up 3 1/8 points for the day.

EXAMPLE 9.4—Dell Computer

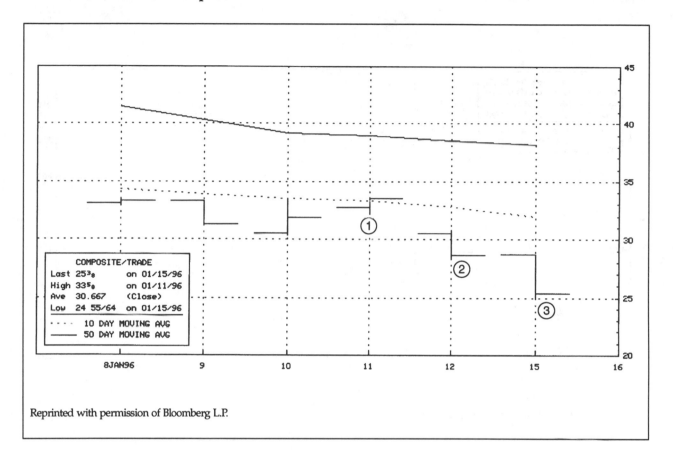

Reprinted with permission of Bloomberg L.P.

Another short setup:

1. A close in the top 25 percent.

2. A close in the bottom 25 percent and under its 10-day and 50-day moving averages.

3. Price persistency at its best. Sell short at 28 1/8, and it closes 2 5/8 points lower, at 25 3/8.

EXAMPLE 9.5—Semiconductor Index

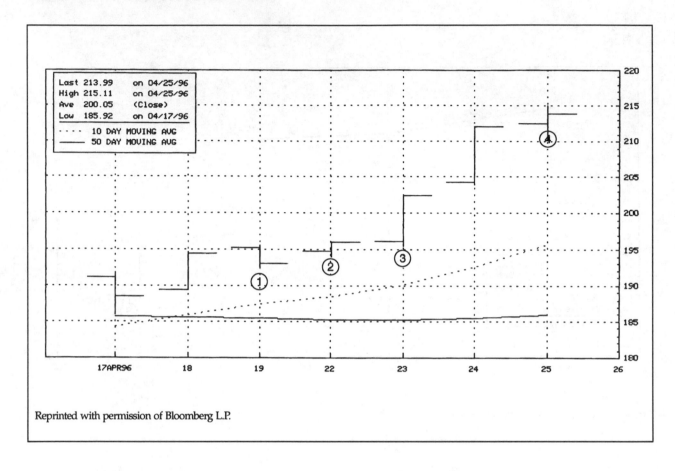

Last 213.99   on 04/25/96
High 215.11   on 04/25/96
Ave 200.05   (Close)
Low 185.92   on 04/17/96
···· 10 DAY MOVING AVG
—— 50 DAY MOVING AVG

Reprinted with permission of Bloomberg L.P.

This setup works especially well in sector indices as I have found that sectors tend to exhibit price persistency even better than individual stocks. I believe it is because once the institutions decide to buy into a market sector, it takes a while for them all to climb on board and fill their plates.

1. The Semiconductor Index closes in the bottom 25 percent of its range.

2. The Index closes the next day in the top 25 percent of its range.

3. We go long (via options) in the 196.05 range, and the Index trades more than 6 points higher at the close.

4. The Semiconductor Index trades 12 points higher in three trading sessions.

EXAMPLE 9.6—NASDAQ 100 Index

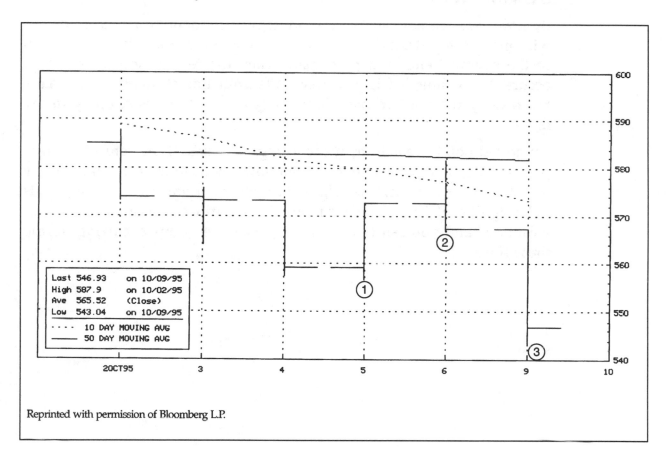

Reprinted with permission of Bloomberg L.P.

The NASDAQ 100 (NDX) is quite volatile and lends itself well to this strategy.

1. A close in the top 25 percent.

2. A close in the bottom 25 percent and under the 10-day and 50-day moving averages.

3. The NASDAQ 100 drops over 20 points for the day from our short entry!

SUMMARY

By now, you see how simple this strategy is to identify and to trade. As with most of my strategies, we risk a small amount, trade in the direction of the overall trend, and participate when the resumption of the trend occurs. Even though I like to day-trade with this strategy, I will many times carry the position overnight, especially if it closes strongly in my favor.

An added point needs to be made as regards 180's. If the setup is accompanied by a 60-day new high or new low, I will more than likely carry the position overnight. The follow-through the following morning tends to be significant. This double combination identifies persistent strength or weakness, and you can find some of your better gains occurring during these times.

PART TWO

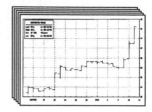

ANCILLARY STRATEGIES

• •

The next seven strategies are my back-up strategies. Most are just as profitable as the main strategies, but they tend to occur less often.

Give extra thought to chapter 16, "Putting Pieces Together." This chapter discusses when multiple signals occur, and I have found these occurrences to be my most profitable.

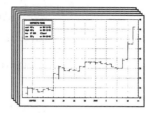

CHAPTER **10**

GILLIGAN'S ISLAND

* *

An empty bag cannot stand upright.

—Ben Franklin

"Gilligan's Island" is a setup I use to trade short-term gap reversals. A gap is nothing other than a market that opens higher or lower than the previous day's high or low.

Gaps are usually caused by a news event that occurs before the markets open. A report of better than expected earnings, or a brokerage house recommendation, causes stocks to gap higher. Poor earnings, lowering of a brokerage house opinion, etc., causes stocks to gap lower.

Gilligan's Island is used to exploit the good news bulls and the bad news bears of the world. I have noticed over the years the number of times stocks will gap to new highs on great news, or gap to new lows on bad news, only to reverse shortly thereafter. Since not all gaps reverse, I set out to isolate the elements of price action that best forecast such a turn. After much research and testing, I found that the Gilligan's Island does it nicely.

With a Gilligan's Island, I ideally want an uptrending stock to gap higher and then reverse. I then look to climb aboard the next day for the ride down. Most times this reversal is short-lived, but occasionally the reversals identify an intermediate- to long-term high and the profits are significant.

Here are the rules:

FOR BUYS

1. A stock must gap open to a new two-month low. The bigger the gap the better.

2. The stock must close at or in the top 50 percent of its daily range and equal to or above the opening.

3. The next day only, buy 1/8 above today's high.

4. **Risk 1 point.**

5. Carry the position overnight if it closes strongly.

FOR SHORT SALES

1. A stock must gap open to a new two-month high. The bigger the gap, the better.

2. The stock must close at or in the lower 50 percent of its daily range and equal to or under the opening.

3. The next day only, sell the stock short 1/8 under today's low.

4. **Risk no more than 1 point.**

5. If the stock collapses, carry the position into the next morning. It will probably follow through.

EXAMPLE 10.1—America Online

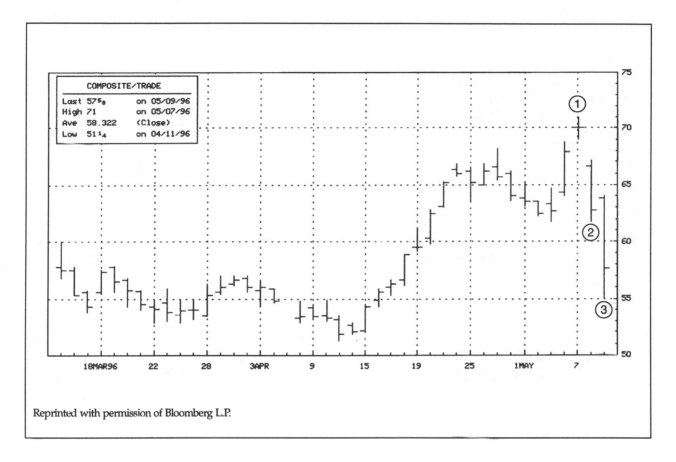

Reprinted with permission of Bloomberg L.P.

1. America Online gaps to a two-month high, closes at its opening price and in the lower 50 percent of its range.

2. The stock opens under the previous day's low and a short sale is triggered at 66 5/8. Our initial protective stop is at 67 5/8.

3. The stock trades as much as 11 5/8 points below our entry.

EXAMPLE 10.2—Pairgain Technologies

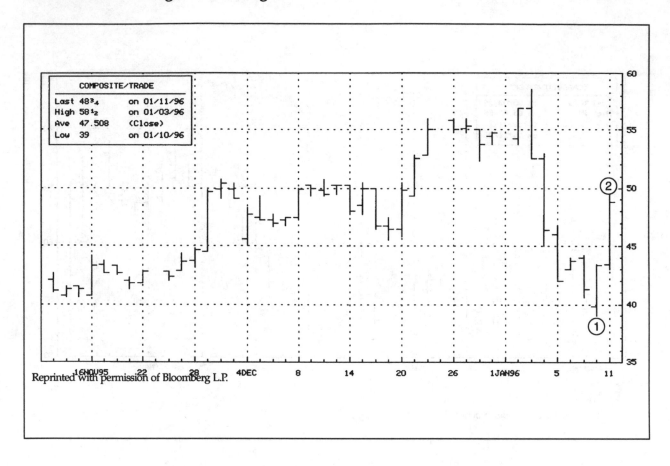

COMPOSITE/TRADE
Last 48³₄   on 01/11/96
High 58¹₂   on 01/03/96
Ave 47.508 (Close)
Low 39   on 01/10/96

Reprinted with permission of Bloomberg L.P.

1. Pairgain Technologies gaps lower to a two-month low and reverses.

2. We buy at 43 5/8, 1/8 above yesterday's high, and the stock climbs intraday over 6 points above our entry.

EXAMPLE 10.3—Electronic Arts

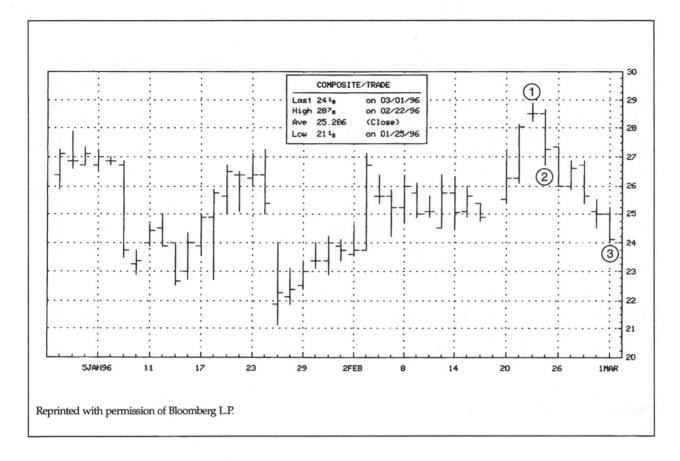

Reprinted with permission of Bloomberg L.P.

1. Electronic Arts gaps to a two-month high and closes at its opening price and in the bottom half of its range.

2. We sell short at 28 1/8, 1/8 under yesterday's low. Our stop is at 29 1/8, 1 point above our entry.

3. Electronic Arts loses more than 15 percent of its value over the next week.

EXAMPLE 10.4—Netscape

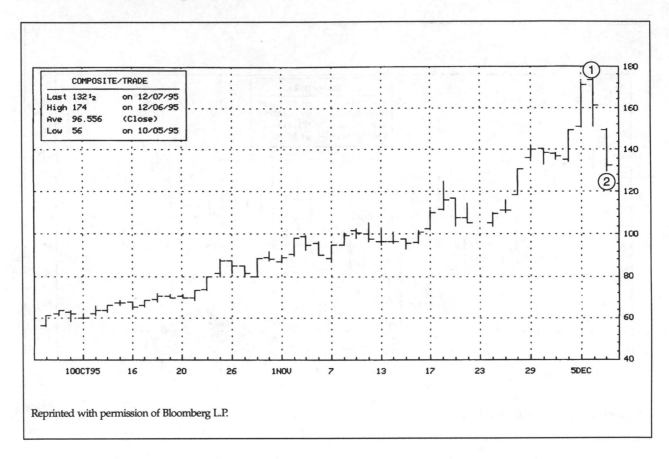

Reprinted with permission of Bloomberg L.P.

1. Netscape Communications gaps open to a new 60-day high, closes in the bottom half of its range and under the open.

2. The stock opens at 149 1/2, under the previous day's low, and we are short. We risk 1 point with our stop at 150 1/2. As you can see, the reversal is sharp as the stock collapses to 132 1/2, 17 points under our entry.

EXAMPLE 10.5—Netscape

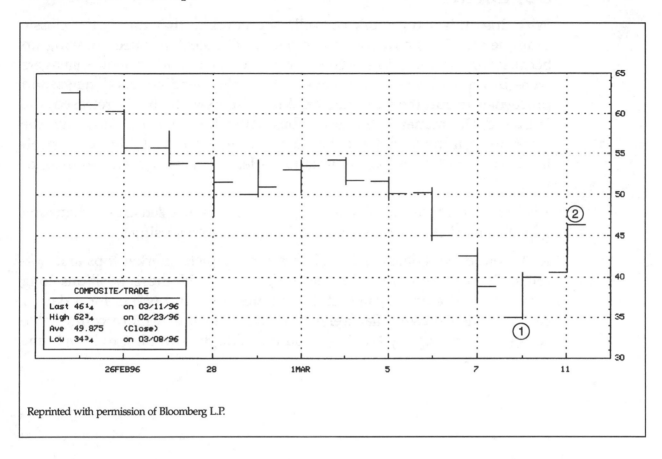

Reprinted with permission of Bloomberg L.P.

Here is Netscape on the buy side a couple of months later (reflects 2-for-1 stock split).

1. Gaps down to a two-month low and reverses.

2. Buy at 40 5/8. Closes at 46 1/4.

SUMMARY

Why does this setup work so well? My guess is that this is the classic example of, "Buy on rumor, sell on news." The stock has been moving up because of the anticipated good news. Analysts and money managers were being whispered information about the pending good news and proceeded to run the stock higher. When the news is finally released, the "in the dark" money is the last to buy. After these weak hands own the stock, the "in the know" money starts hitting the bids, taking their profits. This profit-taking usually lasts for at least a few days and sometimes longer.

Also, in classical technical analysis jargon, this is in a sense an exhaustion gap. The market makes its last final lunge before reversing.

As I mentioned, Gilligan's Island occasionally picks market tops and bottoms. Even though you may be tempted to hold these positions long term, I would advise against it. Most times the setup works for a day or two and then the original trend resumes. I am much more comfortable consistently taking my few points off the table than waiting to hit a home run.

CHAPTER **11**

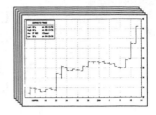

BOOMERS™

• •

Weakness indulged equals greater weakness.
Strength exerted equals greater strength.

—Carlos Casteneda

From time to time a stock in an uptrend or downtrend will pause and have a "quiet period" These quiet times are often followed by explosive moves. While traders use many different ways to identify these quiet periods, I use only one and I call the setup "Boomers." Boomers are fairly rare, but when they do occur, profits can be substantial.

Here are the rules:

FOR BUYS AND SHORT SALES

1. For buys, ADX must be more than 30 and the +DI more than the –DI, or RS must be 95 or greater.

   For short sales, ADX must be more than 30 and the –DI must be more than the +DI, or the stock must be downtrending strongly.

2. Day two's high must be less than or equal to day one's high and its low must be greater than or equal to day one's low.

3. Day three's high must be less than or equal to day two's high and its low must be greater than or equal to day two's low.

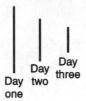

Day one   Day two   Day three

4. For uptrending stocks, on day four only, we will buy 1/8 above the day-three high. Our stop will be 1/8 below the day-three low.

For downtrending stocks, on day four only, we will sell short 1/8 below the day-three low. We will protect ourselves by covering our short position 1/8 above the day-three high.

Let's look at some examples.

EXAMPLE 11.1—SPS Technologies

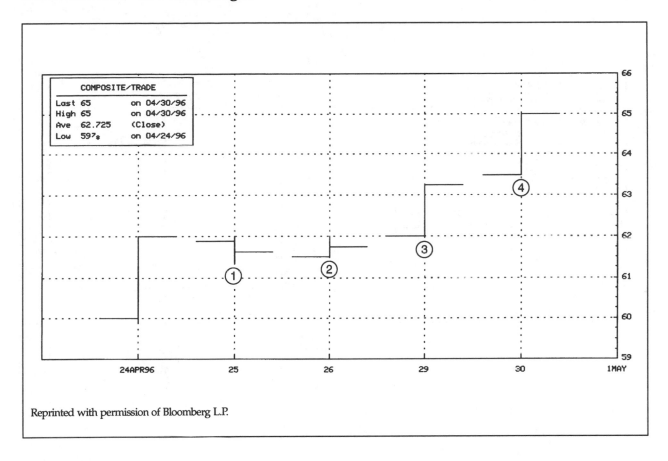

COMPOSITE/TRADE
Last 65 　　on 04/30/96
High 65 　　on 04/30/96
Ave 62.725 　(Close)
Low 59⅞ 　　on 04/24/96

On April 26, 1996, SPS Technologies (ST) has an ADX of 51 and the trend is up.

1. ST has a range whose high is equal to the previous day's high and its low is above the previous day's low (an inside day).

2. The next day its high is less than the April 25 high and its low is higher than the April 25 low (a second consecutive inside day).

3. We buy at 62 1/8, 1/8 above yesterday's high, and our protective stop is at 61 3/8 (1/8 under yesterday's low).

4. The stock closes nearly 3 points above our previous day entry.

EXAMPLE 11.2—Iomega

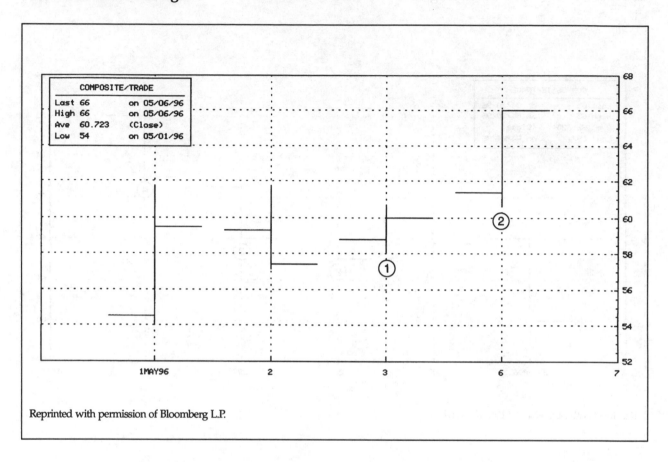

Reprinted with permission of Bloomberg L.P.

1. May 3, 1996—Iomega has two consecutive inside days and the trend, as measured by ADX and +DI, is up. We will buy (tomorrow only) 1/8 above today's high.

2. The stock opens above yesterday's high and we buy at 61 5/8 and our stop is 1/8 under yesterday's low of 58. Iomega closes at 66, 4 3/8 points above our entry.

EXAMPLE 11.3—Gymboree

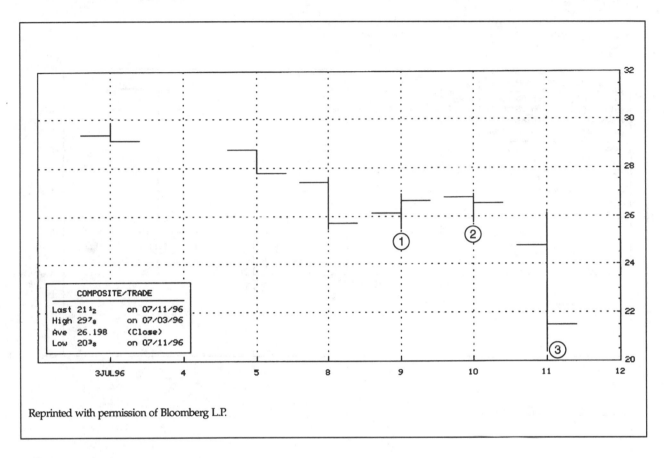

COMPOSITE/TRADE

Last 21^1$_2$	on 07/11/96
High 29^7$_8$	on 07/03/96
Ave 26.198	(Close)
Low 20^3$_8$	on 07/11/96

Reprinted with permission of Bloomberg L.P.

Gymboree has an ADX reading above 30 and its –DI reading is greater than its +DI reading, signifying a downtrend.

1. Inside day.

2. Second consecutive inside day.

3. Sell short at 24 3/4 (the opening price) and trades to as low as 20 3/8.

EXAMPLE 11.4—Nine West Group

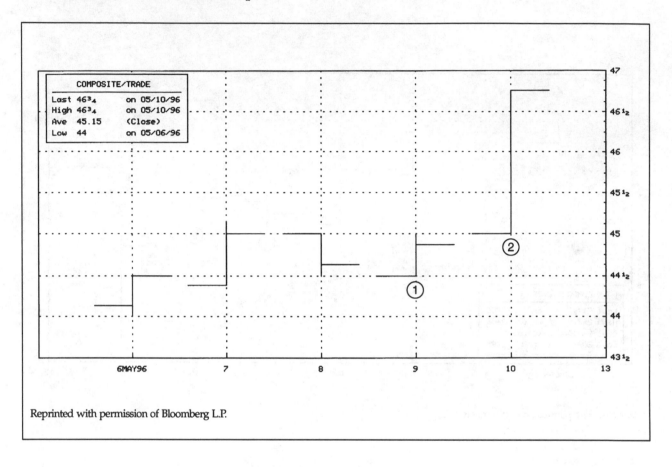

COMPOSITE/TRADE

Last	46³₄	on 05/10/96
High	46³₄	on 05/10/96
Ave	45.15	(Close)
Low	44	on 05/06/96

Reprinted with permission of Bloomberg L.P.

1. Nine West Group has two consecutive inside days and is trending higher.

2. We enter above the day-two high and the stock closes at the high of the day.

EXAMPLE 11.5—Proxim

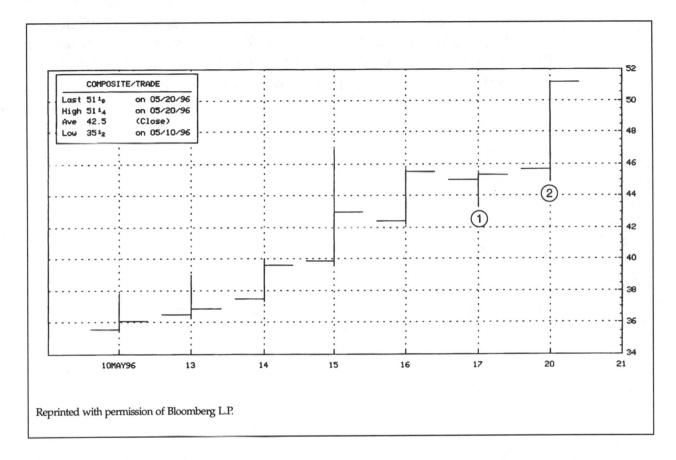

COMPOSITE/TRADE

Last	51 1/8	on 05/20/96
High	51 1/4	on 05/20/96
Ave	42.5	(Close)
Low	35 1/2	on 05/10/96

Reprinted with permission of Bloomberg L.P.

1. Proxim has two consecutive inside days, the ADX is above 30, and the +DI is greater than the –DI.

2. Our buy stop is triggered on the opening at 45 1/2 and the stock explodes 5 5/8 points higher, to 51 1/8.

SUMMARY

Boomers are simple-to-trade, low-risk, high-reward setups. They identify strongly trending stocks that are resting for a few days before resuming their trend. Even though they are fairly rare, I always try to be aware of them as they tend to be high percentage trades.

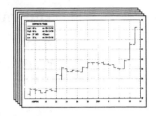

CHAPTER **12**

SLINGSHOTS™

░░

As the instability of systems become more untenable,
the systems of people that survive the crisis become
greater and stronger.

—Ilya Progogine
Nobel Prize Winner
Mathematics

As I mentioned in a previous chapter, we cannot buy every new high and sell every new low and expect to be profitable. We want to identify which breakouts are caused by "the strong hands" and which by "the weak hands." Expansion Breakouts do a good job of telling us which new highs or new lows have the best chance of follow-through. With the Slingshot, I am going to show you the strategy I use to take advantage of breakouts that are initially not "real."

I created the Slingshot strategy after noticing how many times a stock would make a new high (or low) by a small amount and then immediately reverse. The market would then sell off for a day or two and then a second new high (or low) would be made, which turned out to be the beginning of a major breakout. The false breakout *flushes out* the weak hands and the second breakout made a day or two later is made by the strong hands.

This may be difficult to understand, but the rules and examples should clarify it for you.

Here are the rules:

FOR BUYS

1. Day one: Stock makes a new two-month high.

2. Day two: The market takes out day-one low by at least 1/8.

3. Day two or three only: Buy if the stock trades 1/8 above the day-one high.

4. **Risk two points.**

FOR SHORT SALES

1. Day one: The stock makes a new two-month low.

2. Day two: The market takes out day-one high by at least 1/8.

3. Day two or three only: Sell short if stock trades 1/8 below the day-one low.

4. **Risk two points.**

EXAMPLE 12.1—MEMC Electronic Materials

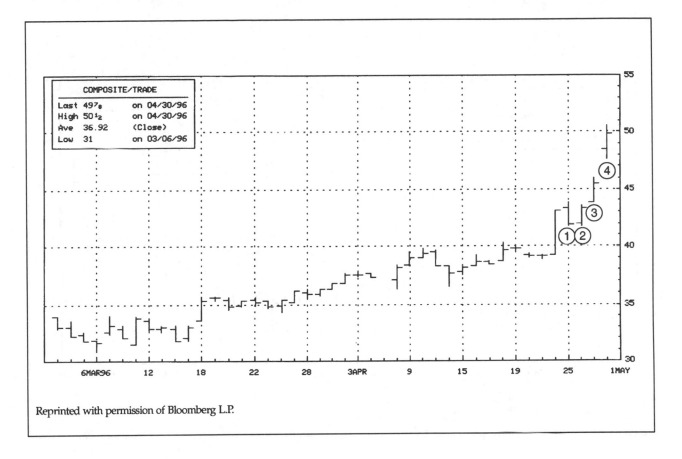

COMPOSITE/TRADE
Last 49⁷₈ on 04/30/96
High 50½ on 04/30/96
Ave 36.92 (Close)
Low 31 on 03/06/96

Reprinted with permission of Bloomberg L.P.

1. MEMC Electronic Materials makes a two-month high and reverses.

2. The stock trades under the day-one low. We will buy either today or tomorrow 1/8 above the day-one high.

3. Stock trades above the day-one high of 43 3/4 and we are long.

4. MEMC Electronic Materials explodes six points in two trading sessions.

EXAMPLE 12.2—IMP, Inc.

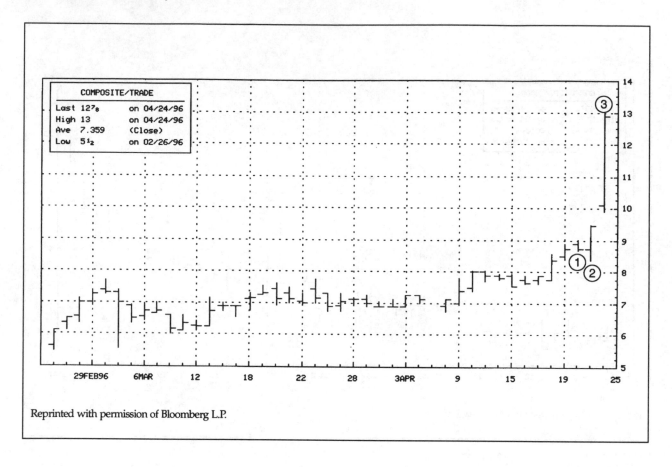

Reprinted with permission of Bloomberg L.P.

Although I am not a fan of low-priced stocks, this example illustrates the power of the setup.

1. IMP sees a two-month high.

2. We trade under yesterday's low and immediately trade above yesterday's high.

3. IMP moves almost 50 percent above our entry within a day.

EXAMPLE 12.3—General Motors

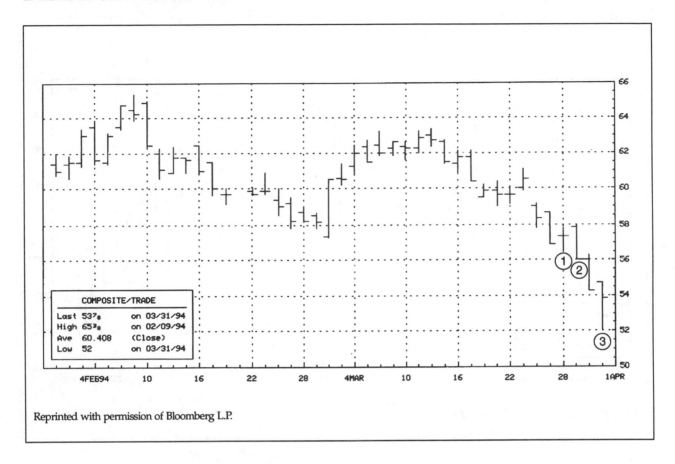

COMPOSITE/TRADE

Last	53⅞	on 03/31/94
High	65⅜	on 02/09/94
Ave	60.408	(Close)
Low	52	on 03/31/94

Reprinted with permission of Bloomberg L.P.

Here's a Slingshot short sale.

1. General Motors hits a two-month low.

2. The stock trades above yesterday's high and then trades under its low. We sell it short at 56 3/8.

3. The stock loses more than 4 points over the next few trading sessions.

EXAMPLE 12.4—Semiconductor Index

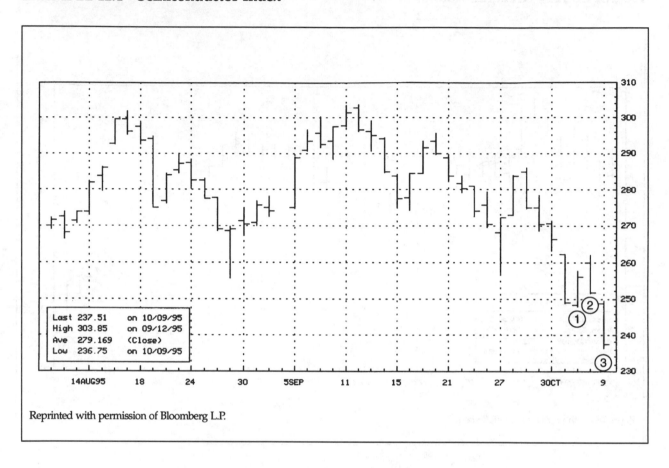

Last	237.51	on 10/09/95
High	303.85	on 09/12/95
Ave	279.169	(Close)
Low	236.75	on 10/09/95

Reprinted with permission of Bloomberg L.P.

This strategy works just as well on stock indices.

1. The Semiconductor Index witnesses a two-month low (day one).

2. The Semiconductor Index trades above the day-one high.

3. The next morning, the Index trades under the day-one low and proceeds to lose 10 points (4 percent!) within a few hours.

SUMMARY

Slingshots are low-risk, trend-continuation setups that do a good job of filtering false new highs and lows. Many times stocks have false breakouts and sucker in momentum players. This strategy allows you to wait for stocks that have flushed out the weak hands before the overall momentum resumes.

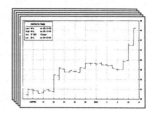

CHAPTER **13**

WHOOPS™

▪ ▪

Deceive the deceivers.

—Ovid

A number of years ago, Larry Williams, the well-known futures trader, created a strategy he called "Oops." The Oops pattern is triggered when prices open above the previous day's high for a potential sell, and below the previous day's low for a potential buy. You buy at the previous day's low plus one tick and sell at the previous day's high minus one tick. This pattern works particularly well with the S&P futures.

I have a twist to the method that can prove to be very profitable with equities. I call it "Whoops!" The main difference is that, by definition, most stocks are not as quickly driven up or down by morning emotion as the S&P futures are. However, many stocks do, in fact, pop up to the upside on the opening without going above the prior day's high. The stock will then immediately reverse, faking out all those who were unfortunate enough to be suckered into the opening move.

For example, on Tuesday, April 9, 1996, Oracle popped up on the open 1/2 point (a "pop-up" is defined as an almost immediate on-the-open rise in a stock). The stock turned to the downside within half an hour and was off as much as 3 1/2 points a few hours later. In this case, the stock was already in a downtrend during the previous session and had closed weakly. Brokerage firms, uncomfortable with Oracle shares in their inventory that they may have been trapped into owning on Monday's close, might have been looking to mark up the stock on Tuesday's open, thus causing the morning price pop-up.

This type of morning reversal action is especially prevalent in trending stocks. For example, when a stock is in a strong downtrend, brokerage houses will manipulate a quick early rise via positive comments, earnings estimate increases, positive opinion changes, etc. (A friend of mine calls them "happy horsesh_t stories.") When this occurs, those who are short get nervous at their first impression of the morning run-up and buy stock to cover their positions. And who will be selling to those shorts? That's right, the brokerage houses that engineered the original pop-up! The pop-up scares the shorts, the brokerage houses clear their inventory by selling to the nervous shorts, and then, as the session advances, the previous day's weakness returns and prices continue their decline. If the stock then goes *negative* on the day, the longs then get nervous. By that point support has become thin and a precipitous move down can be triggered. The brokerage house doesn't care at that point; its inventory has been cleared out at relatively high prices, which it engineered by the early morning action.

How do we profit from a "Whoops" setup? Here are the rules:

FOR SHORT CANDIDATES

1. A stock must be trading under its 10-day and 50-day moving averages.

2. The previous day's close must be below the open.

3. Today's open must be at least 1/4 point above yesterday's close.

4. Sell short at 1/8 of a point below yesterday's close.

5. Maximum initial risk is 1 point.

6. If stopped out, re-enter at the previous entry point (today only).

7. If the stock moves strongly in your favor, move the stop 1/8 of a point below the entry price; a stock that snaps back to being positive on the day could be staging a reversal and you don't want the profit to turn into a loss.

There are no buy whoops. Remember, according to the brokerage houses, stocks only go up, hence bad news is irrelevant.

EXAMPLE 13.1—Diana Corp.

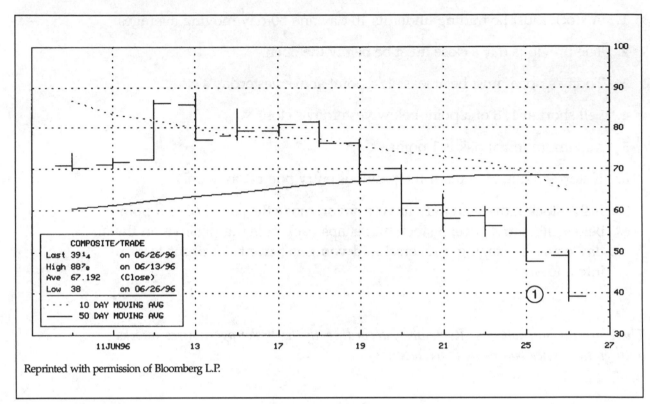

Reprinted with permission of Bloomberg L.P.

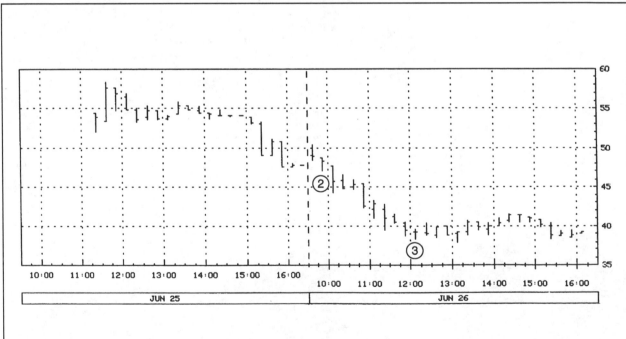

Reprinted with permission of Bloomberg L.P.

The potential for this strategy is best exhibited in this example (see intraday chart).

1. The stock is clearly trading under the 10-day and 50-day moving averages.

2. Stock opens above yesterday's close and reverses. Sell short at 47 5/8, 1/8 under yesterday's close.

3. The stock plummets 8 points in less than two hours.

EXAMPLE 13.2—Chiron

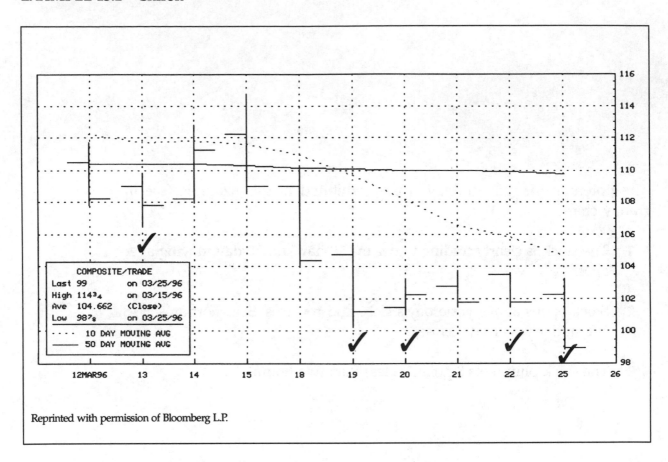

Reprinted with permission of Bloomberg L.P.

In March 1996, Chiron was a terrific example of distribution as it triggered five Whoops setups over a 10-trading-day period. Note how the stock loses nearly 15 percent of its value in spite of the numerous examples of opening strength.

EXAMPLE 13.3—Amgen

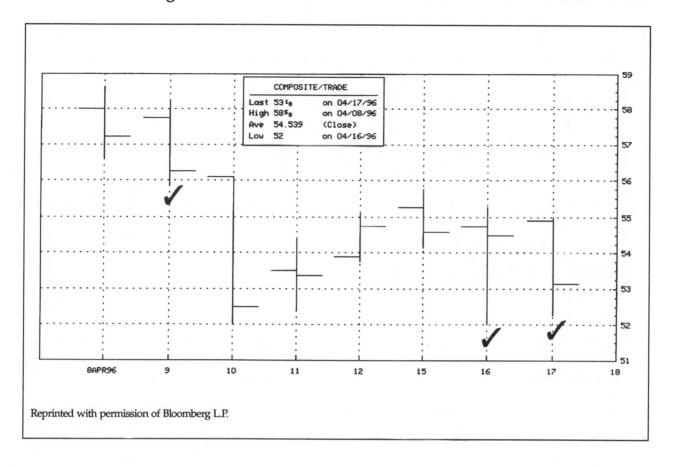

Reprinted with permission of Bloomberg L.P.

Even though the stock market was staging a strong rally, Amgen was going through a short-term distribution phase.

EXAMPLE 13.4—J.P. Morgan

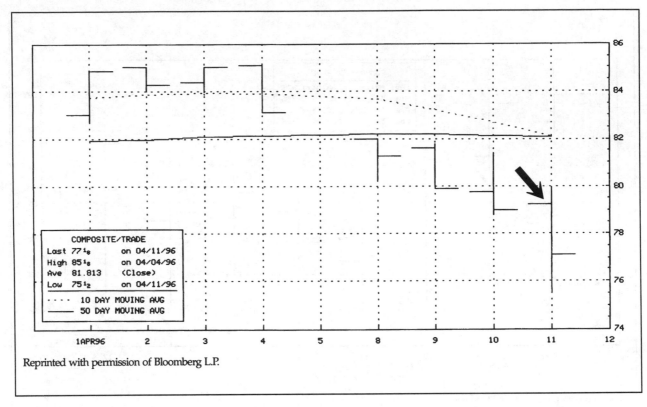

Reprinted with permission of Bloomberg L.P.

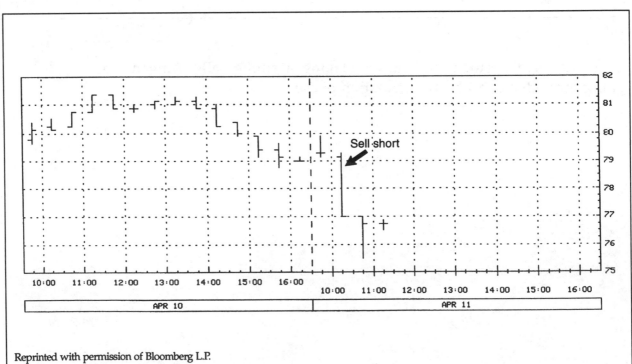

Reprinted with permission of Bloomberg L.P.

Here's an example where J.P. Morgan announced better than expected earnings (see story), but the smart money used it as an opportunity to unload stock.

BBN 4/11 J.P. Morgan 1st-Qtr Net Rises 72% as Trading Surges (Update1)

J.P. Morgan 1st-Qtr Net Rises 72% as Trading Surges (Update1)

New York, April 11 (Bloomberg) -- J.P. Morgan & Co.'s first-quarter earnings rose 72 percent, handily beating analysts' expectations, as revenue from trading stocks and bonds around the world more than doubled.
The nation's fifth-biggest banking company said net income rose to $439 million, or $2.13 a share, from $255 million, or $1.27, a year ago.
The results marked the second consecutive quarter in which J.P. Morgan beat Wall Street's projections. Analysts expected the company, which offers commercial and investment banking services, to earn about $1.71 a share, based on a survey of 15 analysts by IBES International Inc.
``It's a blowout,'' said analyst Raphael Soifer of Brown Brothers Harriman & Co. After a strong January and February for Wall Street, ``March wasn't a very good month, but it didn't seem to bother J.P. Morgan,'' he said.

Morgan said the results were strong across the board. ``Market making, investment banking and investment management all produced substantial gains,'' said Chairman Douglas A. Warner III. Overall revenue rose 25 percent to $1.74 billion from the same period last year.
Operating expenses increased 8 percent from a year ago, while net interest revenue declined 21 percent to $396 million.
The company's shares fell 2 to 77 in early trading.

Trading Revenue Doubles

J.P. Morgan's earnings growth was led by trading revenue that more than doubled to $758 million from $303 million a year ago. The company is one of the biggest traders of stocks and bonds around the world and said higher client activity propelled the increase. Analysts expected the bank to report about $400 million in trading revenue.

SUMMARY

Call me a cynic, but after playing this game for more than 16 years, I believe brokerage houses and market makers have a small amount of larceny in their blood. (If you doubt this, you only need to look at *The Wall Street Journal* on August 9, 1996. There you will get a glimpse of actual conversations among NASDAQ market makers manipulating prices.) It amazes me how many times stocks that are trending down will open higher due to some type of positive comment or event and then immediately reverse to the downside. I believe these positive comments are occasionally made to give either the market makers or brokerage houses a chance to unload unwanted inventory. Therefore, as traders we should heed the words of Sergeant Phil Esterhaus of *Hill Street Blues* who used to say each morning, "Let's be careful out there."

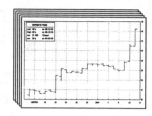

CHAPTER **14**

LIZARDS™

- -

A consistent man believes in destiny,
a capricious man in chance.

—Disraeli

"Lizards" are another low-risk, potentially high-reward reversal pattern. The bar pattern looks like a long tail, which led to my naming it Lizards. I use this strategy strictly for day trading, as I have found it tends to have little significant follow-through value.

Here are the rules:

FOR BUYS

1. Today's (day one) open and close must be in the top 25 percent of its daily range.

Buys

2. Today's low must be a 10-trading-day low.

3. Tomorrow buy 1/8 above the day-one high.

4. Maximum risk is 1 point and if you are not stopped out, sell the position on the close.

FOR SHORT SALES

1. Today's (day one) open and close must be in the bottom 25 percent of its daily range.

2. Today's high must be a 10-trading-day high.

3. Tomorrow sell short 1/8 below the day-one low.

4. Maximum risk is 1 point and if you are not stopped out, cover the short position on the close.

Short Sales

EXAMPLE 14.1—Computer Associates

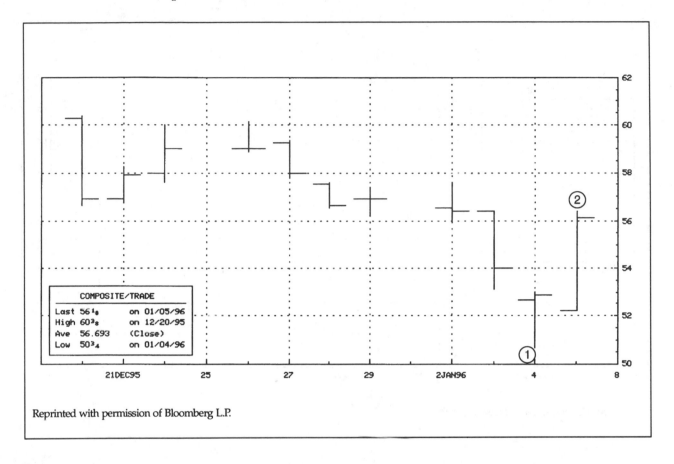

Reprinted with permission of Bloomberg L.P.

1. Computer Associates opens in the top 25 percent of the daily range and closes in the top 25 percent of the daily range after making a 10-day low.

2. We buy 1/8 above yesterday's high of 53 and the stock explodes to above 56 by the close.

EXAMPLE 14.2—Amgen

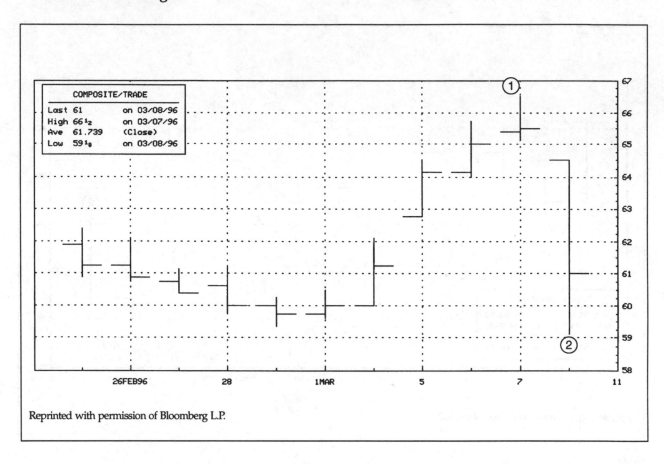

Reprinted with permission of Bloomberg L.P.

1. Amgen makes a 10-day high and its opening and closing prices are in the bottom 25 percent of the daily range.

2. The stock opens under yesterday's price and we sell it short at 64 1/2 before watching it collapse more than 5 points intraday.

EXAMPLE 14.3—Atmel Corp.

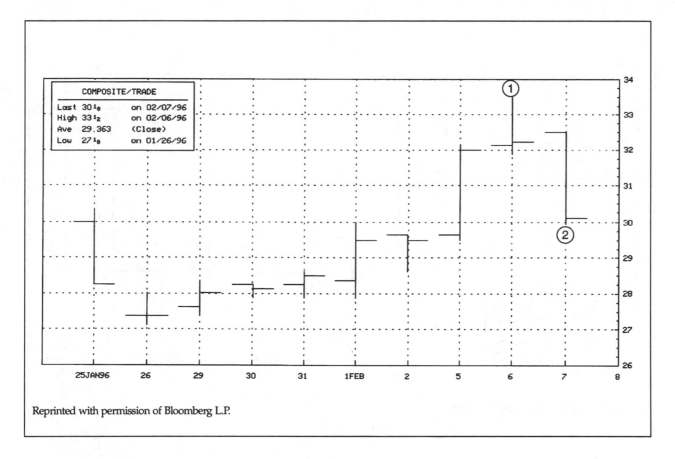

Reprinted with permission of Bloomberg L.P.

1. Atmel Corp. makes a 10-day high and both its open and close are in the bottom 25 percent of the daily range.

2. We sell short 1/8 point under yesterday's low of 31 7/8, and the stock closes 1 5/8 points under our entry.

EXAMPLE 14.4—United Airlines

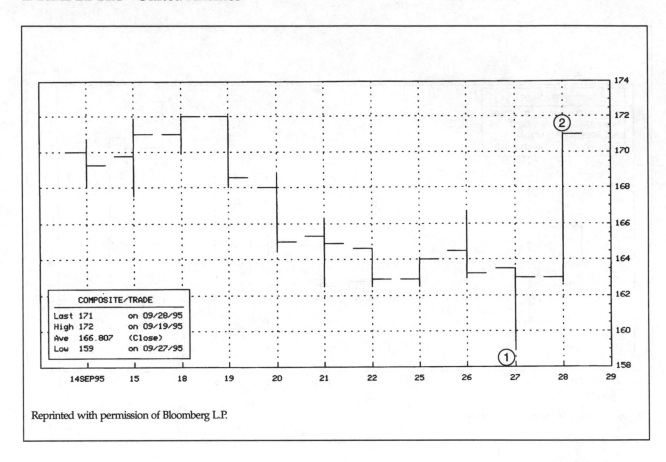

COMPOSITE/TRADE

Last	171	on 09/28/95
High	172	on 09/19/95
Ave	166.807	(Close)
Low	159	on 09/27/95

Reprinted with permission of Bloomberg L.P.

1. United Airlines has a 10-day low, and its open and close are in its top 25 percent of the daily range.

2. Buy at 163 3/4 and the stock lifts off (sorry about that) to 171, 7 1/4 points above our entry.

SUMMARY

This strategy works because the setup is an exhaustion setup. This means that the last buyers or sellers push the stock to extremes before the smart money moves in. Because these markets are making short-term highs and lows, the intraday reversals tend to be fast and furious.

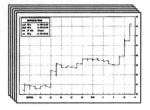

CHAPTER 15

SECONDARIES

· ·

People will buy anything that is one to a customer.

—Sinclair Lewis

Trading secondaries is the lowest-risk strategy I have. Where else can I find a method where a brokerage house basically guarantees me that the most I will lose is a few ticks on a trade?

As you probably know, secondary offerings occur when publicly traded companies decide to sell more stock. They then hire one to five brokerage houses to place the stock with investors. Sometimes (and this is where we come in) the brokerage houses do too good a job of selling the stock, and they create more demand than there is supply. When this happens, the stock tends to run up in price until this demand is met.

How do we know when this situation occurs? From the following rules:

1. On the weekends, read the upcoming offerings section in *Barrons* and identify the secondary offerings that will be released for the upcoming week.

2. After listing these companies, check the news on a nightly basis and identify which ones are priced to begin trading the next day.

3. The stock must close above its 20-day moving average the night it gets priced. This tells me there is good demand for the stock.

4. If the offering opens 1/4 point or more higher than the offering price, buy! For NASDAQ stocks the *bid* must be at least 1/4 point above the offering price.

5. Place an initial protective stop 1/8 under the offering price. If you are not stopped out, but have a loss, sell your stock on the close. If your position is profitable, you have the choice of selling it on the close or holding it overnight. I have found that offerings that have first-day profits many times follow through for a few more days.

Let's look at a few examples (all were trading above their 20-day moving averages on the evening they were priced).

EXAMPLE 15.1—Wet Seal

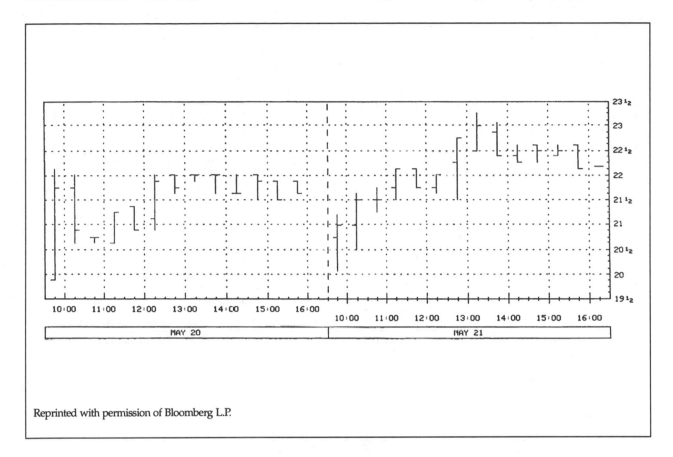

Reprinted with permission of Bloomberg L.P.

On May 20, Wertheim Schroeder prices 3.1 million shares of Wet Seal, Inc. at 20. The next morning, the stock opens at 20 1/2 bid, 20 3/4 offer, and we buy at 20 3/4. If the stock trades under 20, we will sell our position. In this example, Wet Seal trades down to 20 1/8 before the buying comes in and the stock closes at 22 3/16 for the day.

EXAMPLE 15.2—Physician Reliance Network

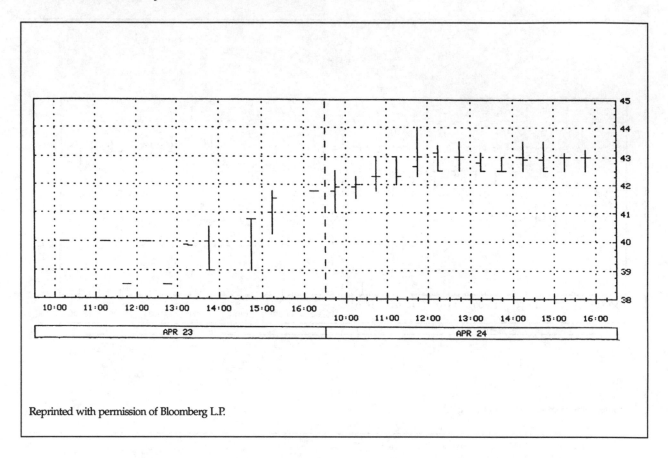

Reprinted with permission of Bloomberg L.P.

Smith Barney prices 2.6 million shares of Physician Reliance Network at 40. The stock opens at 41 bid–41 3/4 offer the next morning (April 24), and we pay 41 3/4. The stock trades to as high as 44 before closing at 43 bid.

EXAMPLE 15.3—Garden Ridge Corporation

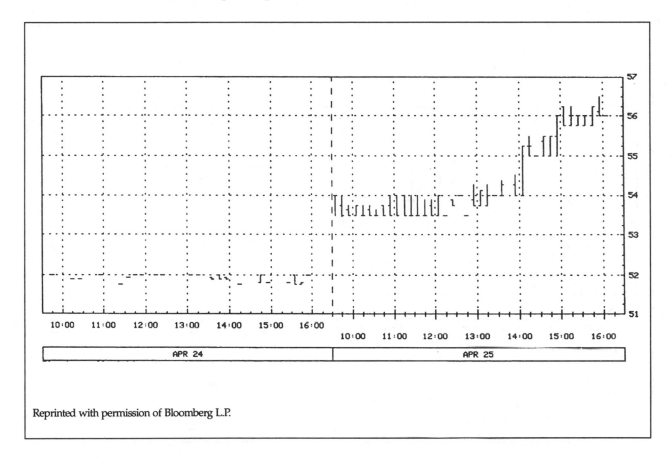

Reprinted with permission of Bloomberg L.P.

Garden Ridge Corporation, a home accessories company, has its offering priced at 51 3/4. The next day, the stock explodes open at 54 and closes 2 points higher at 56.

EXAMPLE 15.4—Renaissance Solutions

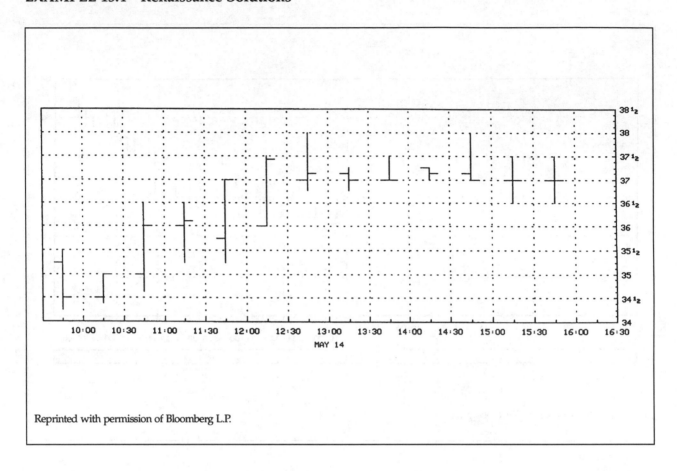

Renaissance Solutions' offering is priced at 33 1/2. The stock opens at 34 3/4 to 35 1/4 and, after a very brief sell-off, climbs to as high as $38 a share. (Also, an Expansion Breakout buy signal was triggered shortly after we purchased the stock. You will learn to put pieces like these together in the next chapter.)

SUMMARY

Why does this work? Because occasionally there is so much excitement about the offering that the demand exceeds the supply. Why? The underwriter has oversold the deal and there is at least a short-term unfilled demand for the stock. I also know the underwriter will be attempting to protect their initial buyers at the price of the offering. I will therefore place my stop 1/8 under the offering price (protection price). Many times, though, the opening price is the low of the day and the stock is off to the races. Again, low-risk, potentially high reward.

Why wait for an uptrending stock offering to open higher? Because of supply and demand. A stock only trends higher ahead of its offering because there is too much demand from institutions and not enough supply offered by the company. This means that the brokerage house has done one hell of a job selling the attributes of this company to its customers. As it comes closer and closer to the offering date, the word begins leaking out that there is not enough stock for the demand. The institutions then begin to satisfy their demand by buying in the open market. Why don't I buy before the deal when I see this? Because there is too much room for manipulation, and I would rather see the stock open at least 1/4 point above its offering price. This tells me my analysis is correct and the stock has a good chance of moving higher. Also, I know that the lead brokerage house on the deal will protect me from disaster in case I am wrong. They certainly do not want to see the deal trade under its offering price the first day of the offering. This means all of their clients will have a loss, and this is too embarrassing. Therefore, they will keep a protective bid for stock at the offering price.

I only hold the stock for a maximum of a couple of days when I trade this strategy. I have found that the stocks tend to lose steam after that.

Before we move forward, I need to mention that this is a bull market strategy. During bear markets, secondary offerings tend to dry up, and when this occurs we put the technique in the closet until the market heats up again.

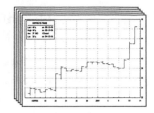

CHAPTER **16**

PUTTING PIECES TOGETHER—The Most Important Chapter

● ●

History repeats itself in the stock market.
Many price patterns and price consolidation structures
that stocks form are repeated over and over again.

—William O'Neil

This chapter is simple and to the point. ***The best way to increase your profits using the* Hit and Run *strategies is to trade stocks that have multiple same-day setups all pointing in the same direction.*** For example, a 180 combined with an Expansion Breakout is a powerful signal. Now Step in Front of Size and guess what? You're probably going to make money and, potentially, damn good money.

Before we look at a few examples, let's briefly discuss the predicament of conflicting signals, i.e., a same-day buy and sell signal. I'll keep the answer short: *Stay out!* Why mess with conflicting signals? This game is tough enough without the noise. Only trade when the signals point in one direction. This advice alone will keep your percentages high enough to give you a fighting chance to win at this game.

Here are some examples of multiple signals pointing in the same direction.

EXAMPLE 16.1—Mossimo

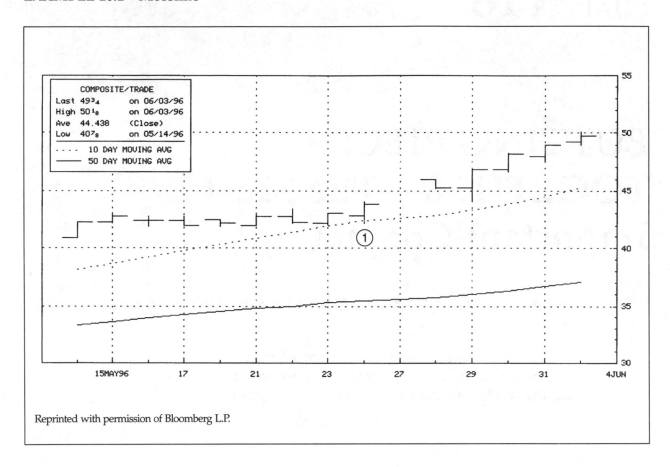

1. On May 24, 1996, Mossimo triggers both a Slingshot buy and a 180 buy before rising nearly 7 points over the next six trading sessions.

EXAMPLE 16.2—S&P 500 Index

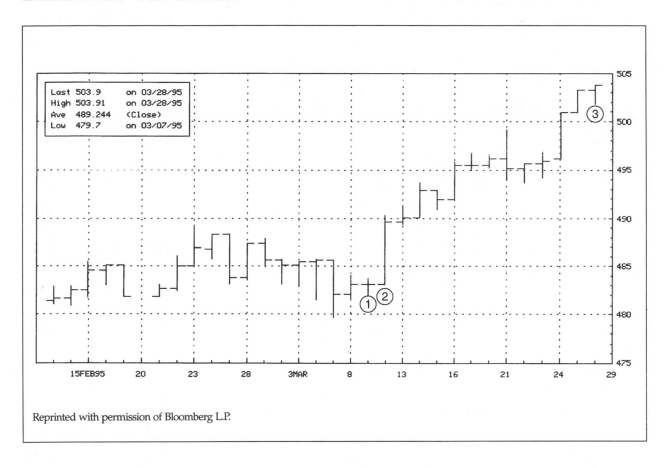

Last 503.9   on 03/28/95
High 503.91   on 03/28/95
Ave 489.244   (Close)
Low 479.7   on 03/07/95

Reprinted with permission of Bloomberg L.P.

Here is an example of back-to-back daily buy signals.

1. A Boomer to the upside (ADX is 47 and the +DI is greater than –DI).

2. Expansion Breakout as the market explodes to the upside.

3. The S&P moves 20 points higher in three weeks.

EXAMPLE 16.3—MRV Communications, Inc.

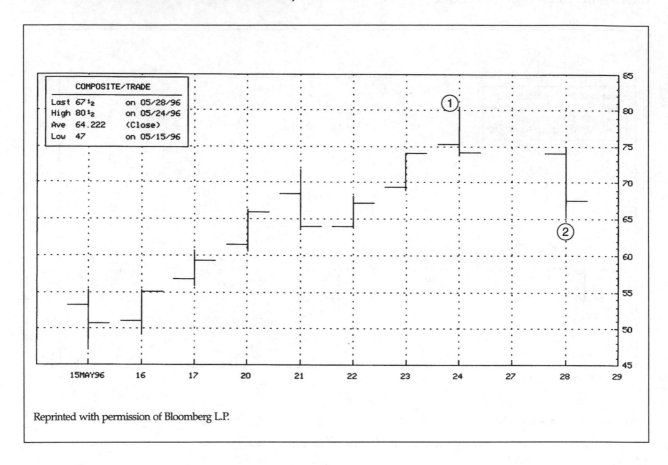

Reprinted with permission of Bloomberg L.P.

1. May 24, 1996—MRV Communications has a Gilligan's Island along with a Lizard sell.

2. The following trading day, the stock drops 9 points intraday.

EXAMPLE 16.4—Delta and Pine

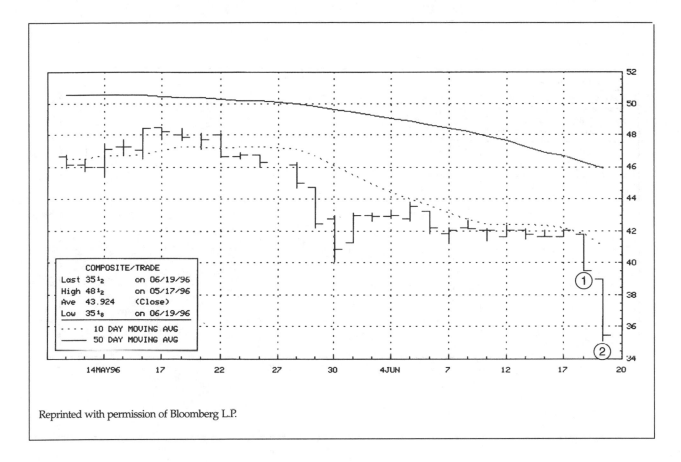

COMPOSITE/TRADE
Last 35½   on 06/19/96
High 48½   on 05/17/96
Ave 43.924   (Close)
Low 35⅛   on 06/19/96

···· 10 DAY MOVING AVG
── 50 DAY MOVING AVG

14MAY96   17   22   27   30   4JUN   7   12   17   20

Reprinted with permission of Bloomberg L.P.

Delta and Pine's implosion over the summer of 1996 leads to a nice two-day combination.

1. A Boomer sell signal is triggered in the morning. At the close, a 180 and Expansion Breakdown sell setup exists.

2. Another sell-short signal is triggered and the stock continues to get nailed.

EXAMPLE 16.5—Global DirectMail Corp.

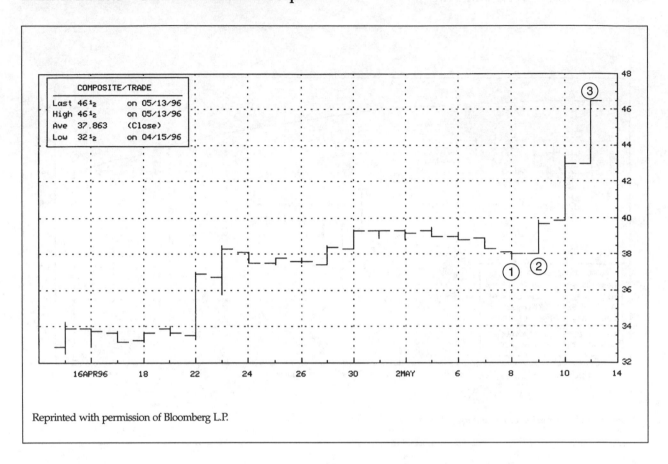

COMPOSITE/TRADE

Last	46½	on 05/13/96
High	46½	on 05/13/96
Ave	37.863	(Close)
Low	32½	on 04/15/96

Reprinted with permission of Bloomberg L.P.

1. A 1-2-3-4 buy . . .

2. Further confirmation by an Expansion Breakout (increase position size).

3. A solid 8 point profit for a couple days' work.

EXAMPLE 16.6—MLHR Equity

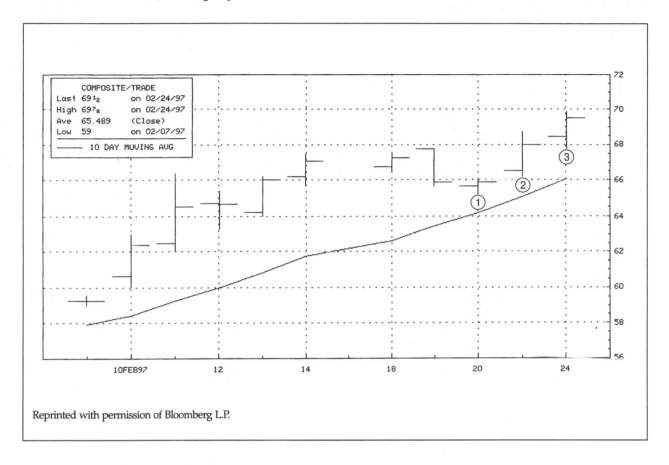

Reprinted with permission of Bloomberg L.P.

It is rare to get three signals at the same time, but when it occurs, the odds are greatly stacked in our favor.

1. A 180 and a 1-2-3-4 setup. Notice also that a Slingshot buy signal will also get triggered if we take out the February 19 high.

2. The 1-2-3-4 and 180 get triggered on the opening and the Slingshot triggers near the close.

3. The stock continues to trade higher.

EXAMPLE 16.7—3COM

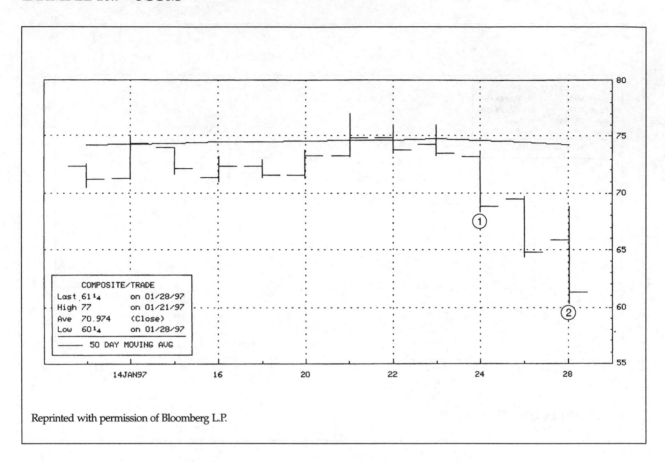

COMPOSITE/TRADE
Last 61¼   on 01/28/97
High 77   on 01/21/97
Ave 70.974   (Close)
Low 60¼   on 01/28/97
——— 50 DAY MOVING AVG

14JAN97   16   20   22   24   28

Reprinted with permission of Bloomberg L.P.

1. On January 24, 1997, 3COM has both an Expansion Pivot and an Expansion Breakdown. This means both the breakout players *and* the institutions who play off the 50-day moving average will be alerted to the stock.

2. Within two days, the stock loses 10 percent of its value.

EXAMPLE 16.8—Ethan Allen

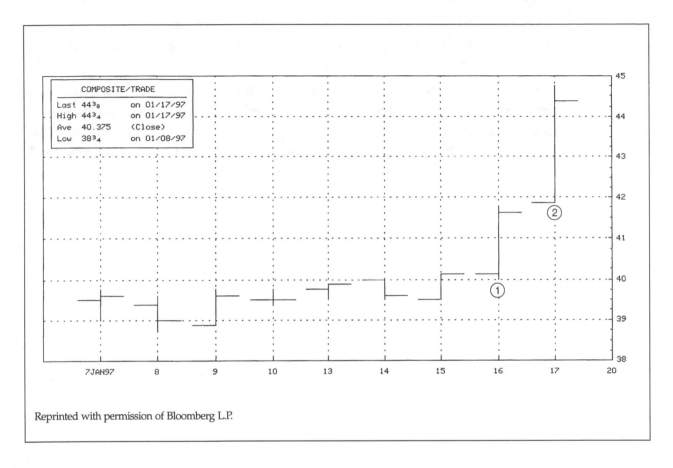

COMPOSITE/TRADE

Last	44³₈	on 01/17/97
High	44³₄	on 01/17/97
Ave	40.375	(Close)
Low	38³₄	on 01/08/97

Any setup combined with Stepping In Front of Size is extremely powerful.

1. Ethan Allen has an Expansion Breakout.

2. The buy signal gets triggered at 40 1/4. Within 18 minutes the stock is trading at 42 5/8 with 5,000 shares bid at that price. One minute later the bid is raised to 42 3/4 for 5,000 shares and two minutes later, there is 10,000 shares bid for at 43. This breakout has attracted desperate buyers and, when you see entry signals combined with panic buying or selling, you should become more aggressive as they usually lead to solid gains.

SUMMARY

By waiting for multiple same-direction signals you are stacking the odds on your side. These setups tend to be high percentage to begin with and, when combined, the chances of success are even greater.

When I get multiple signals in the same day I tend to increase my position size. This means that if I were to normally trade 1,000 shares on an individual setup, I will trade between 1,500 and 3,000 shares on the multiple setup. Obviously, this increases my risk, but the trading results I have experienced from these occurrences justifies taking this risk.

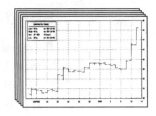

CHAPTER **17**

WALKING THE TALK: A WEEK OF HIT-AND-RUN TRADING

. . . .

Our doubts are our traitors,
And make us lose the good we oft might win
By fearing to attempt.

—Shakespeare

I thought it would be informative and fun to keep a diary of a week of actual trading. I promised myself I would begin this diary the first week after completing the text of the book. I hope to show the good as well as the bad and I will let the chips fall where they may.

You will note that I am a discretionary exit trader. This means I often get out of my profitable positions based on my instincts. I have found that experience, and experience alone, is the best teacher when it comes to exiting a trade.

Sunday, June 9, 1996

I expect the market to be quite volatile for at least the beginning of the week. On Friday, the unemployment report showed strong growth and the bond market instantly collapsed. The S&P 500 futures opened limit down (12 points) and, incredibly, closed higher for the day. It looks like the great bull market of the 1990s has at least a few more weeks of life in it.

My hit list reflects the market's strength. It is overwhelmingly made up of strongly uptrending stocks. In fact, I cannot find any names for down-trending stocks *vis-à-vis* ADX and relative strength. I'm sure I will have some short sales as the week goes on, but in the meantime I will go where the action is. A number of names on my list are familiar to me and have been profitable to trade over the recent weeks. The only new names, names I haven't traded before, are NRL, MST, and CCU.

Before finishing my work, I check the overnight futures markets for the S&Ps, bonds, and currencies and find there is a slight bias to the upside.

Monday, June 10, 1996

Monday morning: The S&Ps are called to open slightly higher and bonds are trading a few ticks above Friday's close. There are no significant news events for any of the stocks on my hit list.

9:30 A.M.	The stock and bond markets open flat. Qualcomm (QCOM) is the first trade of the week. The stock closed on Friday with a 180 to the upside, trades 1/8 higher than Friday's close and I buy at 52 1/4. My stop is at 51 1/4.
9:35 A.M.	HBO and Company (HBOC) is a favorite name of mine to trade. It is on Navellier's list and has provided me with good profits so far this year. The stock has a Lizard buy, and I am filled at 128 3/4.
9:41 A.M.	Another 180 triggered. Rain Forest Cafe (RAIN) triggers a buy and I go long at 48. I'll protect myself with a stop at 47.
9:55 A.M.	Lots of action on the buy side for the morning. Norrell (NRL) has a buyer (or two?) at 51 3/8 and again at 51 3/4. My guess is this is someone who wasn't filled from Friday's explosive upside move and is beginning to panic. I immediately step in front of him and buy the stock at 51 7/8. I'll protect myself by selling at 51 1/4 if it reverses. HBOC is beginning to move.

Symbol	ADX > 30 *or* RS ≥ 95		10- and 50-Day Moving Average	Average Daily Volume < 200,000 shares (NYSE & ASE only)	Trend U = up D = down	Setup
TNL	✓	✓	>	✓	U	1-2-3 Navellier
GYMB	✓		>		U	
AMER			<		D	
NRL	✓		>	✓	U	
SIH	✓		>	✓	U	1-2
MGX	✓	✓		✓	U	
CSCC	✓	✓	>	✓	U	
CCU	✓	✓	>	✓	U	
HBOC			>		U	Lizard Navellier
CYS	✓	✓	>	✓	U	
WHC	✓	✓	>		U	1-2
MST	✓	✓	>	✓	U	
AMAT			<		D	
REY	✓		>	✓	U	
PMS	✓	✓	>	✓	U	
CUBE			<		D	
RGR	✓		>	✓	U	
CHK	✓	✓	>	✓	U	1-2 Navellier
TOM	✓		>	✓	U	
RAIN	✓		>		U	
FLH	✓	✓	>		U	Navellier
QCOM	✓		>		U	180

9:59 A.M.	HBOC explodes to 132 and I'm gone. I make 3 1/4 points in less than 30 minutes. Now you know why I am fond of this stock. As I mentioned, where to take profits is very subjective. When a stock moves 3 1/4 points, though, in less than half an hour, I lock it in.
10:00 A.M.	Size again. Technitrol (TNL) has a 180 buy on the opening at 39 3/4 (which I missed) but luckily I see the buyer and I get filled at 40 1/2.
10:05 A.M.	RAIN is reversing and my protective sell stop at 47 is hit for an immediate 1 point loss. Ouch!
10:20 A.M.	Norrell has exploded to the upside and I take off half my position at 54 and the other half at 54 3/8. My profit is nearly 2 1/2 points in 25 minutes.
10:50 A.M.	The market is not following through to the upside as I had expected, but it doesn't seem to be hurting me. My newfound friend in TNL has panicked and has taken the stock higher. I sell half my position at 42 1/8 and the other half a few minutes later at 42 5/8. As Richard Dreyfus said in the movie *Let It Ride*, "I'm having a good day!"
11:45 A.M.	The day has slowed but RYC has a buyer. I step in front of size and buy at 74.
12:30 A.M.	Qualcomm is going nowhere. I sell at 52 1/4 and scratch the trade. Ideally, I want positions to be profitable for me immediately. When they are not, there maybe something wrong and I don't wait around to find out what it is.
3:32 P.M.	I sell out half my RYC at 75 1/8 for a 1 1/8 profit.
3:59 P.M.	I will keep the other half of RYC. The stock finishes strong and has a 180 setup, and I am comfortable holding it overnight.
Summary	Even though the stock market was quiet, I have a good day. I make six trades with five being profitable. As profitable as the day is, I realize it's only Monday and I must keep things in perspective.

Tuesday, June 11, 1996

9:40 A.M.   My first short position of the week. Fila (FLH) triggers a Gilligan's Island sell at 96 3/8, and I am filled on the first uptick at 96 1/8. My stop is at 97 1/8, and I will watch this stock closely as it has the potential to move a few points in a matter of minutes.

10:46 A.M.   A persistent buyer shows up on Chesapeake Energy (CHK). I step in front of 5,000 that is bid for at 85, and then 85 1/8, and I get filled at 85 1/2. I will risk 5/8 with a stop at 84 7/8.

10:57 A.M.   Fila has dropped more than 1 1/2 points from my short and begins to uptick. Time to take the first profit of the day and I buy at 94 7/8, netting a point and a quarter.

12:23 P.M.   CHK is trading up a point and I decide to lock in the 1 point gain by selling half at 86 1/2.

12:38 P.M.   CHK shows a seller of size at 86 3/4 and I sell my other half at 86 1/2.

Summary   One very quiet day! Days like today can be dangerous because you can get yourself into trouble looking for action. I have done this in the past, and it takes willpower not to do it in the future.

Wednesday, June 12, 1996

Slept poorly last night. I hope it doesn't spill over into my trading. If I worked for a big company I could probably go on cruise control for the day and ramp back up tomorrow. Unfortunately, with this job, cruise control means I don't get paid.

The Consumer Price Index report and Book-to-Bill ratio are excellent and should help stocks a little.

12:03 P.M.   Yesterday's quiet period spills over into today. I came into the day still long RYC. A bid for 5,000 shares at 75 disappears (no trade, and either the buyer changed his mind or the specialist knows something). I immediately get out at 74 3/4 and it proves to be the right move. The stock closes at 72 5/8. As you have heard me say, sometimes you're better off lucky than smart.

12:20 P.M.	HBOC splits 2-for-1 and a Gilligan's Island short sale is triggered at 63 5/8. I get filled on the uptick at 63 5/8.
2:56 P.M.	A Boomer is triggered on RGR at 52 5/8 and I buy. My stop is at 51 1/2.
3:20 P.M.	HBOC trades down and I cover half my short at 62 3/8.
Close	I keep half my HBOC short position and my RGR position overnight. I hope I sleep better tonight so I'm not brain-dead tomorrow.

Thursday, June 13, 1996

The market looks to be very quiet this morning as the S&Ps are called to open slightly higher.

9:59 A.M.	I short AMER on a Whoops at 46 13/16.
12:36 P.M.	The Boomer on RGR is working and in addition, the stock catches a persistent buyer. I step in front of him and buy a second position at 53. Even though the market is down, this stock doesn't seem to care. (I call these stocks torpedoes, as in "Damn the Market, full speed ahead!")
12:54 P.M.	I short Gymboree (GYMB) on a Lizard sell at 35 3/16.
1:11 P.M.	SIH attracts a buyer and I step in front of him and go long at 53 1/4.
1:15 P.M.	America Online is moving against me and I get stopped out with a 1 1/16-point loss. Not only am I the high trade for the day, but the stock immediately moves back down after I cover my short. To say this ticks me off is an understatement.
3:53 P.M.	RGR is trading at 53 7/8, and it's time to cash in half my position with a solid profit.

Close   I go home long RGR and SIH, and short GYMB (1/2-point profit). The day is profitable but I will show you something negative. Fila's Gilligan's Island from the other day took the stock down to 89 1/2,* 5 3/8 points under where I covered. This is the painful side of my Hit and Run methodology, but it is one I am willing to accept. In spite of this, I am again profitable for the day and I am looking forward to locking into a profitable week tomorrow.

* The stock traded to as low as 81 3/8 the next week.

Friday, June 14, 1996

9:44 A.M.   Wackenhut (WHC) triggers a 180 buy and a 1-2-3-4 buy. The signal price is 37 5/8 but the stock opens at 38 1/4, and I buy.

9:45 A.M.   Amazingly, I have not had a single secondary offering buy signal for the week until now. CCU opens at 84 1/4 (priced at 84) and has a buyer of at least 100,000 bid at that price. I immediately step in front of him and get filled at 84 5/8. This is a rotten fill, but I remember one of the traders interviewed in the book *Market Wizards* stating that "the worse the fill, the better the move will be," so I bite my tongue. My stop is at 83 7/8, 1/8 under the offering price.

10:02 A.M.   WHC trades up to 40 and does an about-face. I move my stop to 39 and get filled shortly thereafter for only a 3/4-point profit.

10:44 A.M.   Now I know why that guy is a "Market Wizard." CCU trades up to 86 before a large seller offers stock. I sell half my position at 85 1/2.

11:42 A.M.   I cover half my Gymboree Lizard short at 34 1/4.

2:38 P.M.   The market looks horrible and I would prefer not to carry many (or any) long positions into the weekend. I sell my remaining CCU at 85 1/2 for a 1 point profit.

3:47 P.M.   Gymboree participates to the downside with the stock market and I cover my short and take my profits for the last trade of the week at 33 1/8.

SUMMARY

This is a solid week for the Hit and Run setups. A large proportion of my trades are profitable and, more importantly, my biggest losing trade was only 1 1/16 points. My weekly goal is to net 10 total points from all my trades so this week is especially gratifying.

I need to point out two things that make this week unusual.

1. The majority of my setups were to the long side. Most weeks, I usually make as many short trades as long trades.

2. My original hit list created from Sunday provided me with all my trades. This is rare. Most weeks, I am adding names to the list as the setups warrant. This week's list, though, provided plenty of opportunities from the original names.

The market on the whole had a very sloppy week and a case can be made that distribution is taking place. The Dow lost 38 points and my results are even more gratifying because of this fact. My account has now been profitable for 11 consecutive weeks, and even though I am realistic that losing weeks will occur, I am thankful for my good fortune.

Postscript: My analysis of the market beginning a distribution phase was correct. Over the next five weeks, the market got hit with a very hard correction. The sell-off caused the buy-and-hold boys to give back six months of profits while I had one of my most profitable periods in four years.

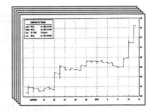

CHAPTER 18

THE CLOSING BELL

* *

A man can be as great as he wants to be.
If you believe in yourself and have courage,
the determination, the dedication, the competitive drive,
and if you are willing to sacrifice the little things in life
and pay the price for the things that are worthwhile,
it can be done.

—Vince Lombardi

You are now armed with my methodology. You now understand why it is critical to be where the action is. You understand the importance of trend and momentum, both to the upside and, just as importantly, to the downside. You realize that a major reason the setups work is because they are used on the correct stocks. You also realize that my methodology risks small amounts and captures small amounts.

Your plan of attack each week does not have to differ much from mine. I trade between 1,000 and 2,000 shares per trade, and I look to make between 1 and 4 points per trade while risking, hopefully, no more than 1 point. My setups average approximately 60 percent winning trades and 40 percent losing. When the week has ended and the dust has settled, I hope to net 10 points. Some weeks I make less, some weeks I lose money (not often, thank goodness), and some weeks I make more. On average, though, the target is 10 points.

As I write this in 1996, thousands upon thousands of money managers and investors hope to be the next Warren Buffet. Unfortunately, most will be poorer with little to show for their efforts when the next bear market hits. Remember, *buy-and-hold* **only works in bull markets!**

My recommendation to you is to trade your newfound strategies slowly. This will allow you to see how each of the setups trade. I can promise you that the Stepping in Front of Size strategy trades vastly different than the Gilligan's Island strategy, etc. Therefore, take it slow and easy and get comfortable with each one before putting your hard-earned capital at risk.

I wish you only the best of luck in your trading endeavors.

Jeff Cooper

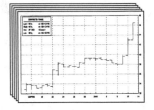

APPENDIX

. . . .

CREATING THE HIT LIST—PART II

I spend approximately one hour each day after the close updating my hit list. This list is important, but please remember it is more important just to be looking at the correct names. Your daily working list of stocks does not have to include *every* name that qualifies by my parameters. It only has to contain a handful of stocks *that are moving*.

The simplest way to look at a universe of potential stocks is to break the list down by indicators for each of the strategies:

1. *Two-month new highs/new lows/range expansion*

    a. Expansion Breakouts

    b. Gilligan's Island

    c. Slingshots

    d. Lizards (10-day)

2. *ADX greater than 30 (± DI or RS 95 or higher)*

    a. 1-2-3-4's

    b. Stepping in Front of Size

    c. Boomers

3. *10/50-day moving average*

   a. 180's

   b. Whoops

4. *50-day moving average/range expansion*

   a. Expansion Pivots

I believe this helps simplify the work and, over time creating, the list will become second nature to you.

Finally, my list is programmed and updated daily on my screen and I am always monitoring the action of these stocks. You will find that a number of names will appear on your list for weeks at a time and, because of your familiarity with these names, they become even easier to trade.

THE BEST WAY TO MAXIMIZE PROFITS

For those of you who are not exclusively day-traders, the following should be of interest to you. I have found from experience that when a stock closes strongly in my favor, it has a higher than normal likelihood of following through the next morning. This means that a long position that closes in the top of its range will likely move higher early the next trading day. I believe this occurs because buyers are not filled and this spills over into the next morning. The same is true for short sales that close near or at the bottom of their range.

Here are two examples to help further this concept.

EXAMPLE A.1—Merck

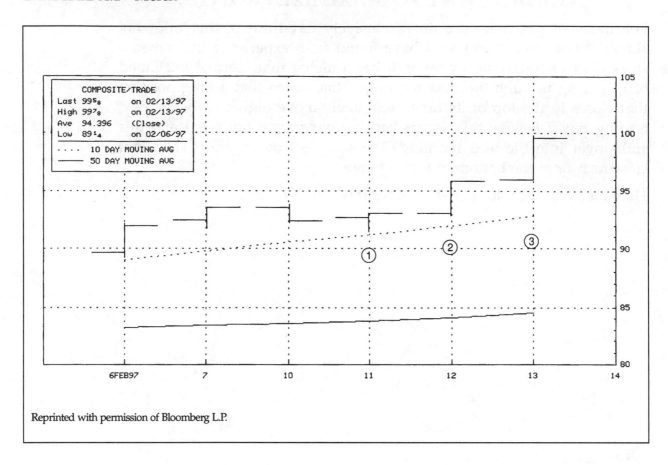

```
        COMPOSITE/TRADE
Last 995⁸        on 02/13/97
High 997⁸        on 02/13/97
Ave  94.396      (Close)
Low  89¹⁴        on 02/06/97
. . . .  10 DAY MOVING AVG
───────  50 DAY MOVING AVG
```

Reprinted with permission of Bloomberg L.P.

1. Merck has a 180 setup.

2. The 180 gets triggered at 93 1/8. Notice how the stock closes at the high for the day of 95 7/8. Unless you need to be out of the position, you should hold at least 1/2 overnight.

3. The buying (momentum!) carries into the next day and Merck closes at 99 5/8. By holding the stock overnight, you participated in an additional 3 3/4 point move.

EXAMPLE A.2—Orion Capital

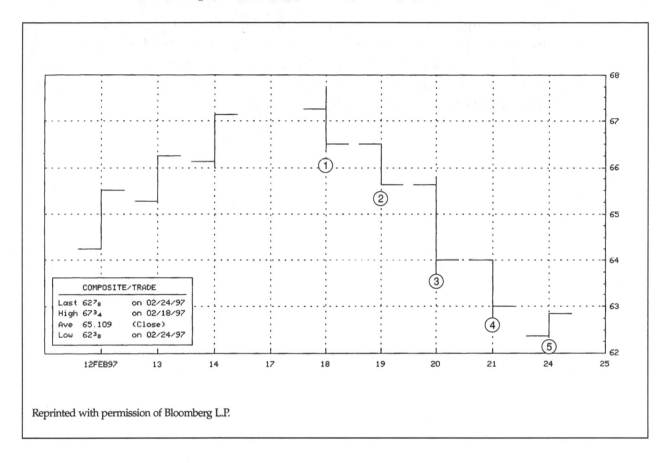

COMPOSITE/TRADE

Last 62⁷₈	on 02/24/97
High 67³₄	on 02/18/97
Ave 65.109	(Close)
Low 62³₈	on 02/24/97

Reprinted with permission of Bloomberg L.P.

1. A Gilligan's Island setup.

2. We are short at 66 1/4 and the stock closes at the bottom of its range.

3. The selling continues and Orion Capital closes again near the bottom of its daily range.

4. More selling and another weak close.

5. A reversal and profits should be locked in.

Finally, when a stock closes poorly (not in your favor), lock in your profits. It is best to put the money in your pocket and go home flat.

HOW I USE TRAILING STOPS

Even though most of my entries are predetermined by mechanical setups, my exits are pretty much discretionary. To help you further, though, I would like to show you how I handle trailing stops and how I lock in profits. Please remember, these are not rules set in stone, but just a guideline to give you an idea of what to look for.

EXAMPLE A.3—Nike

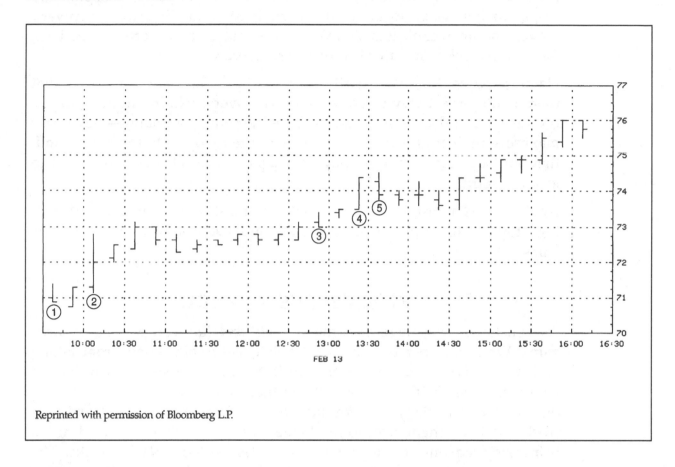

On February 12, Nike had an Expansion Breakout setup.

1. The buy signal is triggered the next morning at 71 3/8 with an initial protective stop at 70 1/4.

2. The stock trades to 72 7/8 and we should immediately move our stop to 71 7/8 to lock in a small profit (and, more importantly, make sure our gain doesn't turn into a loss!).

3. Nike trades to 73 3/8 and we raise our stop another 1/2 point to 72 3/8. Also, at this point, I many times sell half my position as I want to secure a 2 point gain.

4. Another upward move and, with Nike at 74 1/2 and a 3 1/4 point gain, my stop becomes tighter and I move it to 73 3/4.

5. Profit taking comes in and I get stopped out before seeing the stock rise to 76, but the most important thing is I locked in a solid gain.

Some of you may wonder if I would have been better off keeping my stops further away to allow the participation in the further upward move. The answer in this situation is yes, but in many other situations, these stops locked in gains before prices severely reversed.

Having traded for the majority of my adult life, I am convinced that there is no perfect way to exit a trade. The overwhelming number of my friends who are successful traders share the same complaint—they never maximize their trades and it is because of their stops. On the other hand, they are successful because they use stops to protect themselves and to lock in profits.

Again, this is an art, not a science, and the most important usage of trailing stops is to protect your principal and eventually to protect your gains.

RISK VERSUS REWARD

As you have seen, there are times the *Hit and Run* setups lead to large gains. What is imperative to know is that these gains come from taking added risk. The more volatile the stock, the more likely you will have a larger gain when it succeeds, but the more likely you will get stopped out. This is especially true for the NASDAQ stocks. These *"four-letter"* stocks, as I call them, lead to my biggest gains, but they also lead me to being stopped out at a higher rate than less volatile NYSE stocks. The risk you are willing to assume is a personal decision, but please recognize that the more risk you are willing to take on, the higher your pain threshold should be.

CALCULATING ADX

Here is the formula for ADX, +DI, and –DI. I strongly recommend buying a trading software program that does this for you.

INTERPRETATION & CALCULATION
The first +DI and -DI (Directional Indicators) are calculated by summing up the Directional Movements and dividing that by the true range over a period of time (default 14 days).

+DM (Positive Directional Mvmnt)= High Price (today) - High Price (yesterday)
-DM (Negative Direcitonal Mvmnt)= Low Price (yesterday) - Low Price (today)

Days which today's high or low does not exceed yesterday's are ignored.

$$\text{IF } -DM > +DM, +DM = 0. \quad \text{IF } +DM > -DM, -DM = 0.$$

True Range is determined by the largest absolute value of:

1. Today's high - today's low, or
2. Today's high - yesterday's close, or
3. Today's low - yesterday's close.

The +DI measures upward movement and the -DI measures downward movement.

+DI (Positive Direc. Indicator) = summation of { +DM (number of days) / true range (number of days) } * 100

-DI (Minus Direc. Indicator)   = summation of { -DM (number of days) / true range (number of days) } * 100

Subsequent DMs, True Range, and DIs are calculated using a smoothing method once the first +DI and -DI have been obtained.

+DM (today) = +DM(previous point)- (+DM (previous point)/Cycle length) + +DM (today)

-DM (today) = -DM(previous point)- (-DM (previous point)/Cycle length) + -DM (today)

Trnge(today) = Trnge(previous point)-(trnge (previous point)/Cycle length) + trnge(today)

+DI (today) = (+DM(today)/trnge(today)) * 100.
-DI (today) = (-DM(today)/trnge(today)) * 100.

NOTE: "Trnge" denotes true range.

Welles Wilder, the developer of the directional movement system, suggests buying when the +DI rises above the -DI and selling when the +DI falls below the -DI. An equilibrium point is reached when +DI equals the -DI. The stronger the divergence between the two lines, the more the market is trending.

The DX is the directional movement index. It is calculated by dividing the absolute value of the difference of DIs by the sum of DIs and normalizing this by multiplying by 100. The higher the DX, the more directional the movement; the lower the DX, the less directional the movement. Whether the price movement is up or down is irrelevant to the DX; the DX solely measures how up or down the movement is (the amount of the movement).

$$DX = (|(+DI)-(-DI)| / (+DI) + (-DI)) * 100.0$$

The ADX, Average Directional Movement Index, is a kind of moving average of the DX.

Today's ADX = {(Previous ADX * (number of days -1)) + Today's DX} / number of days

The ADXR line, an Average Directional Movement Index Rating, is simply an average of the ADX at the beginning and the ADX at the end of a period:

$$ADXR = (ADX (today) + ADX (today-number of days)) / 2.0$$

An ADXR value above 20 is considered to be a significantly trending market.

WHY I DON'T RELY ON STOCK MARKET ANALYSTS

Over the years, a number of people have asked me why I don't rely on fundamental analysis from brokerage houses. The following may help explain why.

142766 BBN 16:48 Gruntal Probes Bizarre Report by Airline Analyst (Update1)

   Chicago, Aug. 22 (Bloomberg) -- Gruntal & Co. said it is investigating an unauthorized report by its transportation analyst that alleges the U.S. government is involved in a coverup of the cause of the crash of TWA Flight 800 last month, among other conspiracies.
   In a rambling 14-page document sent to the media this week, analyst Steve Lewins also suggests the U.S. government could have prevented the explosion of the Challenger space shuttle in 1986 and says he sleeps with a Samurai sword by his bed because of threats against his life.
   Lewins didn't return calls seeking comment on the report.
   Randy Bradley, Gruntal's executive assistant to the chairman, said Gruntal is reviewing the report, which he said doesn't reflect the views of the firm. Lewins hasn't been fired or suspended, he said.
   ``This was an attempt by Mr. Lewins to write an article or story, but whether it was fiction or non-fiction remains the big question,'' Bradley said. ``In any case, this mailing was done outside the firm and wasn't officially sanctioned by Gruntal.''

                        Killer Parrot

   The document, which is dated Aug. 11, was typed on plain white paper, with handwritten notes scrawled in the margins, and mailed in official Gruntal envelopes.
   The letter ranges across a number of topics. At one point, Lewins says he has received 15 death threats in the past few weeks and his ``killer parrot Tyler stands guard at night.''
   In it, Lewins says the U.S. government is engaged in ``a campaign of disinformation'' to convince the American people that TWA Flight 800 exploded after jet kerosene fumes ignited.
   Lewins says he wrote to officials at Trans World Airlines before the tragedy to tell them that their security at JFK International Airport was lax and left the airline open to terrorist attacks. He says TWA's chief executive, Jeff Erickson, received his letter the morning after Flight 800 exploded, killing 230 people.

Symbolism in Numbers

Flight 800 was chosen by terrorists because the numbers resemble the symbol for infinity, Lewins wrote.

``The zero is like an `O' meaning perfection and infinity representing the holiness of the attack,'' he wrote.

Further, Lewins says the plane was blown up at 13,000 feet because the number 13 represents the 13 original U.S. colonies, the 13 stars and stripes on the original flag and the 13 arrows held by the claw of the American eagle, the national symbol.

He also suggests the Challenger space shuttle was launched at an improper angle with the knowledge of the National Aeronautics and Space Administration, which failed to abort the mission because President Ronald Reagan was set to deliver a major press conference on the launch.

Later, Lewins offers tips for airline safety. He says airlines should give each passenger one liter of water to drink to ward off viral terrorist attacks. He says terrorists can create a virus using farm animals that can be passed to humans.

``The virus starts in the duck, leaps to the pig and, by airborne delivery, infects a person,'' Lewins wrote.

Lewins also says airlines should train their security personnel ``by bringing analysts like me to training sessions.''

Lewins, who has been widely quoted in the media on transportation-related issues, follows airline, railroad and trucking companies for Gruntal.

-- Greg Groeller in the Chicago newsroom (312) 322-7299/br

RECOMMENDED READING

Great investment books are few and far between. Here are some I consider to be the best:

1. *A Fool and His Money*
   John Rothchild
   Viking Penguin Inc.
   $10.95

2. *How to Make Money in Stocks*
   William O'Neil
   McGraw-Hill
   $10.95

3. *Investment Secrets of a Hedge Fund Manager*
   Laurence Connors and
   Blake Hayward
   (800) 797-2584
   $50

4. *Market Wizards*
   Jack Schwager
   New York Institute of Finance
   Available from Traders Press
   (800) 927-8222
   $15

5. *New Market Wizards*
   Jack Schwager
   John Wiley & Co.
   Available from Traders Press
   (800) 917-8222
   $14

6. *Method in Dealing in Stocks*
   Joseph Kerr
   M. Gordon Publishing Group
   (800) 797-2584
   $35

7. *Reminiscences of a Stock Operator*
   Edwin Leferve
   Traders Library
   (800) 272-2855
   $19.95

8. *Stock Market Profits*
   R.W. Schabacker
   Traders Library
   (800) 272-2855
   $21

9. *Street Smarts*
   Laurence Connors and
   Linda Raschke
   M. Gordon Publishing Group
   (800) 797-2584
   $175

10. *Tape Reading and Market Tactics*
    Fraser Publishing
    (800) 253-0900
    $17

11. *Technical Analysis of Stock Trends*
    Edwards and Magee
    International Technical
    Analysis Publishers
    $75

RESOURCE LIST

This sheet has been prepared in order to direct you to services which will facilitate the use of the *Hit and Run Trading* strategies. This list of services represent vendors whom we have dealt with in the past and have had relatively few problems with. This list should not be considered comprehensive in any way. Other services may exist that may serve your purposes just as well, if not better than those listed below. Neither the author, M. Gordon Publishing Group, Cooper Trading, Inc. nor any of its agents warrant the work or services provided by the entities listed below.

CHARTING SOFTWARE

Omega Research (800-422-8587)

Makers of TradeStation and SuperCharts. Both programs chart and analyze price data on an end-of-day and real-time basis. Can be used in conjunction with the *Hit And Run Trading* indicator package that Cooper Trading Inc. offers.

AIQ (800-332-2999)

TradingExpert for Windows is also available for use to analyze price data and offers a wide range of analytical tools. Indicators for the *Hit and Run Trading* systems are not available for this system.

REAL-TIME DATA FEED

Bloomberg (800-448-5678)

A comprehensive real-time quote and news service which also features an extensive collection of analytical tools to assist you with your daily trading. Used by many institutions and priced appropriately.

TrackData (312-553-8722)

Provides real-time quotes through two services, Track/Online (800-367-5968) and TrackData (312-553-8722). Provides the bid/ask lot sizes for use with the Stepping In Front Of Size strategy. TrackData is a more comprehensive real-time quote and news package and requires a dedicated phone circuit to use.

DATA VENDORS

Dial Data (212-422-1600)

Provides end-of-day data on all markets—equities, futures, options, commodities, indexes—for use with charting programs such as TradeStation, SuperCharts, Metastock, AIQ, etc.

PRINT MEDIA

Investor's Business Daily
12655 Beatrice Street
Los Angeles, CA 90066

For a subscription: (310) 448-6000, (800) 831-2525

Louis Navellier's MPT Review
1 East Liberty
Third Floor
Reno, NV 89501

For a subscription: (800) 454-1395

SOFTWARE

FOR HIT AND RUN TRADING I

Omega TradeStation and SuperCharts Owners

Systems, indicators, and paintbars programmed by Stuart Okorofsky from the *Hit and Run Trading* manual by Jeff Cooper. Take five minutes to install these indicators into your TradeStation or SuperCharts library and you are ready to conduct nightly analysis on your database of stocks. This add-on module contains the complete set of indicators and systems for the *Hit and Run Trading* library. It also allows you to create a nightly report of setups that have been triggered from your database of stocks, and look at historical setups that have triggered for a particular stock. Compatible with versions 2.1 and higher of both TradeStation and SuperCharts.

Price—$175

Equis MetaStock Version 6.5 and Professional Owners

We have created a MetaStock add-on module for the Hit and Run Trading methodology. It contains Explorers and Expert Advisors. The Explorer is used to scan portfolios (limited only by the number of stocks in your database) for potential setups. The Expert Advisor will highlight and label potential setups.

Price—$175

FOR HIT AND RUN TRADING II

Omega TradeStation and SuperCharts Owners

We have created an add-on module for TradeStation and SuperCharts. The software identifies the patterns of *Hit and Run Trading II*. It alerts you to daily signals, plots entry and initial stop placement points, and allows you to scan a portfolio for setups. It also includes modules that will help you create the daily Hit List and identify potential candidates for Stepping In Front Of Size on New Highs and Lows™. The above is implemented using TradeStation and SuperChart's indicator and ChartScanner features.

The software comes with a complete user's manual to help you fully utilize the methods.

Price—$175

Equis MetaStock Version 6.5 and Professional Owners

We have also created an add-on module for MetaStock 6.5 and Professional. The software identifies the patterns of *Hit and Run Trading II*. It will scan a portfolio for daily signals and label the bars of the setups. It also includes modules that will help you create the daily Hit List and identify potential stocks for Stepping In Front Of Size on New Highs and Lows™. The above is implemented using MetaStock's Expert Advisor and Explorer features.

The software comes with a complete user's manual to help you fully utilize the methods.

Price— $175

Other Books from M. GORDON PUBLISHING GROUP

HIT AND RUN LESSONS: Mastering the Trading Strategies

JEFF COOPER

175 Pages   Hard Cover $75.00

Do you ever wish you could spend a few weeks looking over Jeff Cooper's shoulders watching him trade? If so, then Hit and Run Lessons: Mastering the Trading Strategies is for you. In it, Jeff Cooper draws from his Daily Learning Sheets and gives you a blow-by-blow analysis of the actual trading set-ups that he has been trading for the past four years. You'll not only see what Jeff does, but also learn how Jeff thinks when he stalks trading opportunities through Pullbacks, Breakouts, Reversals, Stepping-In-Front-Of-Size, and more.

This book is a must for every trader's collection.

HIT AND RUN TRADING II

Capturing Explosive Short-Term Moves in Stocks

JEFF COOPER

212 Pages   Hard Cover $100.00

212 fact-filled pages of new trading strategies from Jeff Cooper. You will learn the best momentum continuation and reversal strategies to trade. You will also be taught the best day-trading strategies that have allowed Jeff to make his living trading for the past decade. Also included is a special five-chapter bonus section entitled, "Techniques of a Professional Trader" where Jeff teaches you the most important aspects of trading, including money management, stop placement, daily preparation, and profit-taking strategies.

If you aspire to become a full-time professional trader, this is the book for you.

THE 5 DAY MOMENTUM METHOD

JEFF COOPER

61 Pages   Spiral Bound $50.00

Strongly trending stocks always pause before they resume their move. The 5 Day Momentum Method identifies three- to seven-day explosive moves on strongly trending momentum stocks. Highly recommended for traders who are looking for larger than normal short-term gains and who do not want to sit in front of the screen during the day. The 5 Day Momentum Method works as well shorting declining stocks as it does buying rising stocks. Also, there is a special section written for option traders.

THE BEST OF THE PROFESSIONAL TRADERS JOURNAL SERIES

FROM LARRY CONNORS

Market Timing

42 Pages   Soft Cover $39.95

Learn how to determine which way the Dow, S&Ps, and Nasdaq are going the next day. Professional traders often use sophisticated tools and indicators to help them determine market bias for the next day. Larry Connors gives you his best strategies for determining market direction for the next day in an easy-to-understand and easy-to-use format. Learn how Larry exploits the VIX and TRIN indicators to successfully trade the markets. Backtesting results on just one of the strategies contained in this book has yielded a 288 percent return in just four years!

Includes the Connors VIX Reversal I–V, TRIN Reversals, TRIN Thrusts, and Percent Advance/ Decline Indicator (PADI).

Options Trading and Volatility Trading
55 Pages   Soft Cover $39.95

Ninety-seven percent of options traders lose money. Professional trader Larry Connors shares his best options trading strategies with you to help you avoid being just another losing trader. By exploiting stock splits and pricing inefficiencies as well as applying his own strategy, the Connors VIX Reversal, Larry delivers four powerful options methodologies that move the odds decidedly in your favor. In addition, Larry also provides you with the latest research on the little-known, but powerful indicator, historical volatility. From concept to action, Larry explains to you step-by-step how to best use historical volatility to conquer the futures, stock, and options markets.

Includes Trading Volatility with Options, Trading Options with the Connors VIX Reversal, Options on Stock Splits, and Exploiting Over-Priced Stock Sector Options.

Day Trading
44 Pages   Soft Cover $39.95

Everyone who wants to trade professionally must have this book. In it, Larry Connors shares five strategies that will help you become a top-notch day trader. These strategies represent the culmination of over 15 years of trading experience. Larry shows you how to use the powerful ADX indicator to become a winner in the stock market and in the S&Ps. Jeff Cooper also contributes his time-proven Torpedoes strategy to exploit the stock market on an intraday basis. Find out how real traders read the markets during the day.

Includes the 15-Minute ADX Breakout Method, Trading the 15-Minute ADX Breakout Method with Equities, S&P Momentum Day Trading System, Front Running the S&P's, and Torpedoes.

Best Trading Patterns, Volume I
41 Pages   Soft Cover $39.95

Trading is a war and only those traders who are properly prepared will succeed in battle. In *Best Trading Patterns, Volume I*, Larry Connors provides you with an arsenal of short-term trading patterns to successfully trade both stocks and futures. Larry takes you step-by-step through each strategy in this book and defines for you exact entry and protective stop points. If you trade based on gaps, volume, or pullbacks, this book contains the strategies that teach you to successfully trade them all!

Includes The Crash, Burn, and Profit Trading Strategy, Double-Volume Market Top Method, Bottom Reversals, Large-Range Days, Momentum Gaps, Triple-Day Pullbacks, and Turtle Thrusts.

Best Trading Patterns, Volume II
58 Pages   Soft Cover $39.95

If you can't get enough of Larry Connors' time-tested, market-proven, short-term (three- to seven-day holding periods) trading strategies, this is the book for you. Successful trader and hedge fund manager Larry Connors gives you seven potent technical trading strategies to conquer the stock and futures markets. Unlike other trading books that talk *around* trading, Connors' *Best Trading Patterns, Volume II* gives you exact rules for entry along with several illustrated examples to show you how these strategies have traded in the past. This book is designed to get you from reading to trading immediately.

Includes the Spent Market Trading Pattern, 1-2-3-4s, The 8-Day High/Low Reversal Method, 10% Oops, Momentum Moving Averages, Gipsons, and Wide-Range Exhaustion Gap Reversals.

THE 5 DAY MOMENTUM METHOD
DAILY TRADING SERVICE
— For short-term (3 to 7 days) traders!

Trade the Best 5 Day Momentum Method Setups Everyday!

One of the world's top equity traders shares his daily signals with you. Since Jeff Cooper made his 5 Day Momentum Method Daily Trading Service available to traders two years ago, the results have been terrific. Over this period, fax subscribers have participated in some of the biggest point gainers on Wall Street.

For Example:

- Recently, subscribers entered St. Joe Corp (SJP) at 96 3/4. Two days later, the stock closed 18 1/4 points higher.
- Subscribers bought Schlumberger (SLB) and National-Oilwell (NOI). Both stocks were exited within a few days for a combined profit of over nine points.
- Jeff's subscribers bought Atwood Oceanics (ATW) at 113 3/4. Three days later, the stock traded more than eight points higher.

The 5 Day Momentum Method Daily Trading Service Works in Both
Up Markets and Down Markets

Too many traders lose money when the market drops. The 5 Day Momentum Method is structured to not only take advantage of uptrending stocks but also to profit from downtrending stocks. This assures you of participating in both rising markets and declining markets!

For Example:

- Recently, subscribers shorted Merck (MRK) at 90 1/2. The next morning they covered at 82, for an 8 1/2 point profit.

What You Will Receive Each Evening as a Subscriber

The 5 Day Momentum Method Daily Trading Service is simple to use. Each evening (5 nights/week) you will receive via your choice of fax or email, Jeff's 1 - 3 best setups for the upcoming day.

His recommendations include:

- The exact entry price
- Whether to buy or sell short
- Where to place your protective stop
- Where to take profits on half your position and on the fifth day where to exit your remaining position.

Price: I month – $175 • 3 months – $450 • 6 months – $750 • I year – $1,250*

Includes a copy of Jeff's audio tape Trading the Stock Market for a Living.

ABOUT THE AUTHOR

Jeff Cooper is a full-time, professional equities trader. A graduate of New York University, he is also the author of *Hit and Run Trading I* (1996), *Hit and Run Trading II* (1998), and *Hit and Run Lessons: Mastering the Trading Strategies* (1999). You can read what Jeff has to say about the market daily at 9:10 A.M. EST at www.TradingMarkets.com.

FREE REPORT
Maximize Your Trading Profits Immediately!

David Landry, TradingMarkets.com Director of Research, has put together a set of simple money management rules to help all traders become more successful in his report *The True Secret to Trading Success: Simple Money Management Rules That Will Make You a More Profitable Trader!*

To obtain this report, send your request along with your name and address to:

M. Gordon Publishing Group, Inc.
445 S. Figueroa Street, Suite 2930, Dept. H1
Los Angeles, CA 90071

Or

Fax your information to 213-955-4242.

Your report will be mailed immediately.